The Developing Child

Recent decades have witnessed unprecedented advances in research on human development. Each book in The Developing Child series reflects the importance of this research as a resource for enhancing children's well-being. It is the purpose of the series to make this resource available to that increasingly large number of people who are responsible for raising a new generation. We hope that these books will provide rich and useful information for parents, educators, child-care professionals, students of developmental psychology, and all others concerned with childhood.

Jerome Bruner, New School for
Social Research
Michael Cole, University of
California, San Diego
Barbara Lloyd, University of Sussex
Series Editors

The Developing Child Series

Children's Talk

Catherine Garvey

Harvard University Press
Cambridge, Massachusetts
1984

This book is printed on acid-free paper, and its binding materials have been chosen for strength and durability.

Library of Congress Cataloging in Publication Data

Garvey, Catherine, 1930-
  Children's talk.

  (The Developing child)
  Bibliography: p.
  Includes index.
  1. Language acquisition.   2. Children—Language.
3. Discourse analysis.   I. Title.   II. Series.
P118.G28   1984   401'.9   83-22536
ISBN 0-674-11634-8
ISBN 0-674-11635-6 (pbk.)

Acknowledgments

I am grateful to the children and their mothers who generously shared their time and talk with me and my co-workers. A number of students and associates assisted in the research described in this book, and in many cases their contributions are acknowledged by their listing as authors in the references. To Kathleen Pike, Gail Rae, Karen Reynolds, and Millie Schwienteck, I take this opportunity of expressing thanks for help in my research and writing. The support of the Spencer Foundation in my study of two-year-olds' talk is also gratefully acknowledged.

Contents

The
Developing
Child

Children's Talk

Two boys, ages 49 and 50 months, have come to the laboratory playroom from the same nursery school class. One boy picks up a large stuffed toy snake and turns toward the other boy.

Boy	Boy
(Waves the snake at his partner.)	
	Help! *(Shouts in mock fear.)* Don't.
It's not a real snake.	
	Well, don't. Stop. Well, stop playing snakes.
I'm 'tending this is a snake. *(Stops moving it and looks at the snake.)* By the way, it *is* a snake.	
	Wait. Make believe/ make believe that's my pet and he never bites me.
'Tend he'll bite me. *(Turns the snake's head toward himself.)* I said, "No" *(speaking to the snake).*	
	Snake! *(speaking to the snake)* No! Don't bite my pal.
(Moves the snake toward the back of the large wooden car.) 'Tend it bited your license plate. 'Tend it was just a little crack.	
	Okay. *(Watches as his partner moves the snake around.)*

1 / The Nature of Talk

The child's first step, first tooth, first word—each is greeted as a momentous event by parents, not for its intrinsic worth, but rather as a harbinger of a long and exciting course of change and accomplishment. In the first step there is the promise of running, skipping, dancing, perhaps pole vaulting, perhaps a chance at the Wimbledon Cup. The first tooth suggests the transition to solid food, visits to the dentist and visits from the tooth fairy, whistling perhaps, and an ever-changing inventory of favorite and detested foods. It is the first word that opens up the most expansive vistas. Ahead lies the rediscovery of all familiar things in their names, the pleasure of nursery rhymes and folk tales, the possibilities of arguing, learning to read, making promises, gossiping, even perhaps making poems or writing legal briefs. Parents, of course, use talk extensively to socialize the child and to induct him* into the social world of his and their community. But it is not only the parents who sense that something of great importance has happened as the first words begin to appear; children themselves become absorbed with this new capacity and begin, usually with considerable enthusiasm, to explore what they can do with words.

* I have used the male pronoun generically because it seemed awkward to do otherwise.

Why do children talk? The ultimate reason is that they are biologically designed to do so. Talking comes as naturally as walking or playing. The immediate reasons for talking are extremely varied. Children talk from a number of motives, for a number of purposes. They talk to share a feeling or impression with others, to influence others and to evoke predictable responses from them; at times children talk to keep themselves company or to help in ordering and understanding their physical and perceptual world; sometimes they talk just for fun and sometimes because talk is an inextricable part of some activity in which they are engaged. And, of course, very often they talk when they are urged, prompted, and encouraged to do so by their caregivers.

The linguist Michael Halliday observed his young son during the period when his vocalizations were assuming consistent phonological form and when he began to exhibit clearly an intention to communicate by means of these forms.[1] Halliday was able to distinguish seven different functions, or uses, of his son's talk, which he took to be models of the child's conception of what talk is for. The first notion to emerge is that of talk as *instrumental*, a means of satisfying wants and needs. Another function is *regulatory*: the child discovers that others seek to control him by talking and that he can also control the behavior of others. The child also senses that one can establish and maintain contact with others by talking; he recognizes the *interactional* function. The child also expresses his individuality in talking; he asserts himself and his own sense of agency, for talking is a field of action in which he can make choices and take some responsibility. Thus talking has a *personal* function, as well. The *heuristic*, or learning, function is exemplified in the perennial questions "why?" and "what's that?"; the child finds that he can use talk to learn about and to describe his world. And talking serves the *imaginative* function of pretend, which may overlap with an aesthetic function (although Halliday does not dwell on this possibility) as the child realizes that he can create images and pleasurable effects by talking. Finally, and perhaps the latest use of talk to appear, is the *representational* function, or talking to inform. Adults, when they think about language, regard it as a means of expressing propositions or as a means of conveying information. They view this as the primary function of talk, but it is hardly the dominant use for the child. The young child displays one or another of these functions at a time in his simple utterances, but during the latter half of his second year, this relatively simple state of affairs becomes more complicated. As the child's talk comes more and more under the control of the grammatical system of his language, he is able to make explicit relations between concepts and to indicate just what it is that he is doing in his talk. He is no longer limited to a single word with perhaps an accompanying gesture, as when he remarks the presence of his clown doll by pointing and saying, "Clown," requesting the doll by reaching and saying, "Clown," or offering it to another child while saying, "Clown" or "Here."

Language both enables and constrains the encoding of experience, and it does so in a highly efficient manner. The unit of linguistic encoding is the clause, which simultaneously organizes a propositional content, indicates the orientation of the speaker to the addressee and to that propositional content, and reveals its relations to prior and/or succeeding clauses. Thus any clause contains propositional content, interpersonal information, and textual information. For example, a speaker can, by selecting from a number of linguistic options in the production of a clause, inform an addressee of some state of affairs and indicate his own attitude about it: "That's a clown" versus "That might be a clown" versus "A clown is what that is." He can also display his attitude toward the addressee and at the same time attempt to influence him: "Give me the clown" versus "Could you give me the clown?" And the speaker can choose his words to link his message with what has been said before: "I like him, too," as a response to the question "I like the clown, don't you?"

How the child gains control of the resources of his language is the topic of the field of language acquisition. A number of excellent books summarize the recent research in this field, and the reader is referred to them for information on the details of linguistic development.[2] The subject of this book is the activity of talking, an activity that grows and changes throughout the life span but shows the most dramatic transformations during early childhood.

Why select talk as the topic of this book, rather than language or communication? First, because children learn language through talking and attending to the talk and behavior of others. Whereas language is an individual acquisition, talk is the public vehicle for acquiring it. Second, because talk depends on skills, knowledge, and motives that originate and continue to develop outside the linguistic system, in interpersonal relations and in other experiences with the social and physical world. Thus almost every aspect of a child's development is reflected in his talk. And although talk is most frequently associated with communication and most frequently occurs in social settings, many children talk when they are alone and when they have no intention of communicating with others.

TALK AS ACTION

Just as talk cannot be isolated from interpersonal relations or from the situation in which it occurs, so it cannot be separated from the intentions of the speakers. When people talk, they are necessarily also performing social acts, and when they listen, they are hearing in terms of social acts. This fact may be quite apparent in the case of acts that are done only or primarily by means of words, such as "I apologize." But no message can be encoded without simultaneously indicating the speaker's intention as to the type of social act or acts that message should represent. This important insight was set forth by the philosopher John Austin in the book *How to Do Things with Words*.[3] He realized that every utterance carries three kinds of significance. First is the locution, the linguistic form that has its linguistic meaning. Second is the illocutionary force, the type of social act the speaker intends. Third is the perlocutionary force, the significance perceived by the addressee, which may or may not coincide with that intended by the speaker.

It is possible to think up a hypothetical proposition consisting of the concepts, *chase, cat, dog*, and then order and relate these concepts to generate a certain type of linguistic structure: *The cat chased the dog*. But if this structure is to be encoded as a message (and thus be spoken or written in a particular situation), it will necessarily carry an illocutionary force. That is, the declarative sentence form, *The cat chased the dog*, might be uttered as a representative, or assertion, which would convey that the speaker believes the message to be true and believes further that the addressee does not know this information. If uttered as a representative, the message can have any number of situated forms, depending on what was said before, for example, "The cat chased the dog"; "She chased him"; "Chased him, she did"; even "She did" or "Yes," in answer to the question, "Did the cat chase the dog?"

The question "Did the cat chase the dog?" or "The cat chased the dog?" conveys another type of illocutionary force, that of a directive. Here the speaker's intention is to convey that he does not know whether the message is true or not, wants the addressee to tell him, and believes the addressee is able and willing to do so. If the speaker's act is successful, the addressee will realize that he has been requested to supply information; if he answers the question, the act has also succeeded in having the desired perlocutionary effect. Perhaps the act fails or misfires in some way, and the addressee says, "Are you asking me or telling me?" In that case the illocutionary force was unclear, although the addressee may have understood the linguistic content of the message. In questioning the first speaker's intention, the addressee indicates that it is the type of act that is in doubt. In doing so he distinguishes between two basic types of social acts.

Language provides a number of words for verbal social acts, including a number of words for acts that differ only very slightly from each other, for example, ask, request, command, order, plead, beg, all of which suggest that the speaker wants the addressee to do something. Austin and, more recently, several other scholars have set up a limited number of categories, or major act types, of what we do with words, attempting to capture the principal distinctions that speakers make.[4] Although the things we do with words have proved to be almost as slippery as the meanings of the words themselves, there is considerable agreement that we do issue and interpret utterances as intended to be directive (the speaker wants the addressee to do something), representative (the speaker believes something to be the case), commissive (the speaker commits himself to a course of action), expressive (the speaker displays a particular feeling or orientation, for example, "I'm sorry" or "Congratulations"), or declarative (the speaker brings about a specified state of affairs, such as, "You're fired").

The several problems in any such classification system derive from the nature of talk and of talkers. First, there is no necessary one-to-one correspondence between the locutionary type and the illocutionary type. Granted, we often use an interrogative form to make a request for information (a type of directive), but we also use interrogatives to perform other types of acts, and we can request information by using a different utterance type, for example, saying after an introduction, "I didn't catch your name." Second, we can combine acts in one utterance, perhaps linking a directive with a commissive—"If you say that again, I'll leave." Third, we can use these acts for shady purposes, to be ironic, duplicitous, sarcastic, and even to be intentionally ambiguous. And we can deny that we intended to insult someone, saying, "But I only asked you a question," thus retreating in a cowardly fashion behind one speech act after achieving another purpose. Fourth, although all utterances can be placed in a few basic categories, it is often the more subtle distinctions, and those made at a higher level of social interaction than the utterance, that are the most salient for speakers. These are the distinctions that are remembered, discussed, reported, and perhaps acted upon. It is usually more important to the participants that the speaker intended to insult the addressee than that he used a directive requesting information, or a representative, or several types in succession. A fifth problem is that very little is known about the perlocutionary effects, the consequences of verbal acts, which are not fully under the speaker's control. If an addressee answers a request for information, then the speaker has achieved the intended perlocutionary effect, but the side effect of being insulted by the question cannot be accounted for within the current theories of speech acts. Finally, and closely related to the fifth problem, the theory of speech acts and the proposed systems of classification have dealt primarily with isolated acts and acts abstracted from the flow of talk. Dependent acts—those that are contingent on preceding acts (responses) or those that anticipate subsequent acts (preparations)—have been neglected, although responses are far more frequent in talk than initiations, and preparations influence the interpretation of the subsequent act.

Despite these problems, the conception of talk as doing has had a profound effect on our understanding of talk, especially that of young children, for they are immediately engaged with doing things with words, even before they have many words at their disposal. And, perhaps an even more important part of the concept is that as children are learning to talk, they are also learning the bases of social action and interaction.

TEXT

The product of talking is a text. Even in its preserved form, in writing or on tape, say, and abstracted from its situation of occurrence, talk displays texture. The parts are interwoven in various ways and connected in differing degrees, a characteristic that has led to such metaphors as "the web of discourse," or "a tissue of lies." The text is held together, the parts linked, often quite redundantly, by a number of tying devices as well as by our sense of the coherence, or relevance, of one part to another. The text in its original form is also closely integrated with its setting. These connections can be represented only partially in a record of talk by adding contextual information to the transcript. For example, we can note that the speaker was pointing to a cup when he said, "That is." Identifying the object in the physical surroundings would be essential to understanding what he meant, but it is obviously not enough to allow us to interpret the utterance. *That* links the talk both to the physical setting and to what another speaker has just said, in this case perhaps, "Nothing is broken." Given the prior utterance and the contextual information, the utterance can be interpreted as meaning, "That cup is broken." But to capture the original coherence of the exchange, a written record would also have to indicate that the word *that* was emphasized by the speaker's higher pitch and volume. Intonation, the prosodic aspect of language, which includes direction and level of frequency, amplitude, and duration, also functions to link the parts of the text.

Our sense of sequential relevance in the unfolding of a text (or its converse, irrelevance, or thinness or breaks in the texture) is created and reinforced by a number of different linguistic and nonlinguistic factors. None of them is quite as influential, however, as the participants' expectation that the persons involved are committed to being cooperative, that each will try to say and do what is relevant and appropriate to the situation and the purpose of the interaction. As H. P. Grice, the philosopher who formulated this "cooperative principle" pointed out, this act of faith holds for any task, whether talk is involved or not.[5] Responsible people are expected to assess what is going on and to contribute accordingly. If you see a person loaded with packages and struggling to open a door, and if you wish to engage yourself in his problem (rather than hurrying past and ignoring it), you open the door and hold it open until he enters; you do not offer him a light or hand him some change. Similarly, if a person asks a question, he expects the addressee to answer. He inspects what the addressee says for its potential as an answer, since in conversation a contiguous remark is usually considered to be contingent. If the addressee's utterance is not apparently relevant—is not an answer, a justification for not answering, an attempt to elicit information needed to formulate the answer, or any other acknowledgment that a question has been asked—the first speaker will try to create relevance by inferring a link between what the addressee said and a possible response to the question. If possible, he will assume that the addressee was being ironic or witty or overly discreet: he seeks a reason for the apparent breach of cooperation. Intentional violation of the cooperative principle is rare, but children often violate the principle accidentally.

Cooperation requires that the participants share a definition of the situation and that each contribute the next appropriate act toward the shared objective. Thus two people must, at least tacitly, agree on what they are doing—changing a tire, giving and accepting instructions, or swapping jokes. Very young children are accustomed to having caregivers join their action lines in play, but even two-year-olds can assess what an adult is doing, if the task is a familiar one. Harriet Rheingold, in a laboratory observation that simulated conditions in the home, found that a majority of the 18-month-old children and almost all of the 24-month-old children spontaneously joined an adult's activity and "helped" to set the table, fold the laundry, dust the furniture, and pick up bits of trash. Their collaborative efforts and their vocalizations clearly indicated that they recognized the adult's goal, knew what actions were called for, and knew when the task was completed.[6] Cooperation in talk also begins to appear before the age of two years. At first children are more likely to speak immediately after an adult's utterance than to initiate talk, but what they say is often not contingent on the adult's speech. They are, however, more likely to produce a relevant response after a question than after an utterance that does not require a reply.[7] At the beginning of a child's conversational life, caregivers not only model cooperative talk by responding relevantly to almost anything the child says, but they work to allow the child to provide a response that is relevant and appropriate to the task or topic.

Coherence.   The texture of talk arises primarily from the ties of relevance created by the participants cooperatively addressing their remarks to the topic or task at hand. Language provides a number of ways to mark relevance and to display both the coherence of the talk and the participants' mutual attention and responsiveness. Coherence, whether between speakers, within one speaker's contribution, or both, leads to considerable redundancy, which, were it not reduced, would rapidly bring talk to a halt. An example, taken from a discussion by two three-year-old girls engaged in "playing house," illustrates how talk addressed to a topic of joint concern builds up redundancy and at the same time reduces some of the accumulated verbal burden. What the children do not say, but nonetheless imply and understand, is indicated in parentheses:

Karen	Lisa
They won't let me iron real clothes. I'll pretend I'm ironing clothes.	
	Yes, they do (let you iron real clothes).

Karen	Lisa
No, they don't (let me iron real clothes). They really don't (let me iron real clothes). They really won't allow me (to iron real clothes).	
	They allow me (to iron real clothes).

Neither child identified the persons indicated by *they*, but each accepted those persons as individuals who could and would permit or forbid the children's actions. (Such "imprecision" is, of course, acceptable in adult conversation, too; if something can be taken for granted, it usually is.) Once Karen had established the contrast between ironing real clothes and pretending to iron clothes, both children could and did assume that the new information was shared and could be reduced in the surface form of the messages. Had the shared information not been reduced by means of rule-governed omissions, or ellipsis, as in the present example, or by some other linguistic means for indicating without actually repeating the previously encoded information verbatim, the talk would have required more effort and patience than even normally repetitious three-year-olds could muster. The job of encoding was lightened by partial ellipsis of the shared material, which was fully retrievable. However, the process is not completely automatic; note that Karen and Lisa understood that Lisa's first elided message meant "let *you* iron" and Karen's first elided message meant "let *me* iron." Also Lisa's first message, although contiguous to Karen's message, "I'll pretend I'm ironing clothes," was actually contingent on Karen's prior message, "They won't let me iron real clothes." Finally, although Karen's insistence may seem a bit repetitious, she does use another linguistic tying device to vary the form of her message; she paraphrases "let me" with "allow me," a change Lisa notices and adopts. In this example linguistic cohesion interacts in several ways with the substance and responsiveness of the exchanges to provide an integrated text.

Within a text, information, or the content of messages, is continuously changing. First, new elements are introduced, which may then be modified, repeated, or manipulated in some way. But as the previous example illustrated, once introduced, new elements are likely to be reduced in surface form on the very general principle in talk that familiarity breeds brevity. As talk continues, old elements may drop out, and new ones may be introduced; sometimes an earlier element is reintroduced. Throughout this process the participants must keep track of what information is new to a partner and what is old, or given, and thus retrievable, either from the partner's knowledge store, from a prior point in the text, or from the situation. They observe the terms of what Herbert Clark has called "the given-new contract."[8] The speaker signals, using one or more of a variety of linguistic devices, what part of the message is to be understood as new, and he makes less prominent the part assumed to be given. Trusting in the cooperation of the speaker, the addressee dutifully attends to the new information and searches, in the text or context, as appropriate, for the information to flesh out the old, or given, material.

The linguistic devices that signal the given or new status of information in a message and the placement of the given information are quite specific. When children fail to use these devices correctly, they may be assuming that the addressee already knows a particular piece of information. Thus a child who runs into his petless house and announces "The dog bit me" does not take into account that his mother does not know he was playing in a neighbor's yard. The neighbor's dog, a painfully given fact in his own memory, is not present in his mother's awareness. Children make this type of error more commonly than adults, and caregivers are quite consistent in introducing new information to a child explicitly and checking to be certain that it is shared before treating it linguistically as given.

Speakers can, of course, treat as known, or given, information that has not been previously introduced and that is not available to the addressee from any source outside the message and the rules governing the meaning and use of language. Information can be presupposed. A presupposition is a state of affairs that must obtain before another state of affairs (a meaning, a logical proposition, a speech act) can be valid, true, or appropriate. The word *father* carries with it the information that the individual referred to is male and adult and that he has literally or figuratively one or more offspring. Similarly, the message "I know what Helen got for her birthday" carries the presupposition that Helen got something for her birthday along with the message that the speaker knows what that something is. A clever speaker can take advantage of this potential of talk to register more information than just what is asserted, knowing that the addressee will attend primarily to the new and focal information. A suspicious mother might ask an unwary child, "How many cookies did you have before dinner?" She presupposes, although the child had not admitted to it, that he had had some cookies, but she inquires directly only about the quantity. In order to ask, "How many cookies did you have?" the speaker must either know (or guess) in advance that the addressee has had any cookies or must treat that possibility as a fact while ostensibly asking only about the specific number.

Indirection. Another common characteristic of talk, and one which is almost as difficult for children to learn to control as it is for theoreticians to explain, is indirection. Language provides a number of ways for speakers to be indirect. For reasons having to do primarily with the speakers' social relationships (see Chapter 4), they do not always choose the most direct, simplest, or clearest way of formulating a message. If a speaker wishes an addressee to perform action X (feed the dog, perhaps, or dry the dishes), he can choose the direct formulation, saying, "Do X," or he can choose from a number of indirect formulations that can convey directive force, his choice being influenced by politeness, deference, familiarity, even by the difficulty of the action or its probable cost in time or effort to the addressee. He can say "Will you do X?"; "Would you mind doing X?"; "X needs to be done"; "I hope you can find time to do X"; "Could I ask you to do X?" He can even hint without mentioning action X precisely, leaving the addressee to cooperatively infer what the speaker wishes to have done: "Rufus looks hungry" or "Where's the dog's supper?" If it is the addressee's standing obligation to feed the dog, either that assertion or that question can, and probably will, be interpreted as directive in intent. An indirect formulation may seem more polite or at least less intrusive or bossy, and it is not necessarily inefficient. First, the interpersonal orientation conveyed by the indirect form may be quite as important to the participants as the desired action. Second, an indirect formulation often includes information relevant to understanding the underlying proposition and its relation to the speech situation. Third, if the addressee is attentive and willing to collaborate, the indirect formulation may effectively accomplish two communicative acts at the same time.

An example will illustrate these three potentials of an indirect formulation. Two people are going to visit a mutual friend. As they drive, one asks the other, "Do you remember Mary's address?" The other replies, "Yes, it's 1524 Pine Road." The first speaker does not ask, "What is Mary's address?", although presumably he wants that information. His more indirect formulation permits the other to admit, if necessary, to having the same poor memory as the speaker. Further, the speaker's formulation directs the other to search for information he once had. And finally, the speaker receives the information he presumably wants, the exact address, as the other both responds to the indirect formulation by saying, "Yes" (meaning "I do remember") and, without further prompting, goes on to provide the information. If the addressee of an indirect formulation is either unskilled or uncooperative (or possessed of a particularly crude sense of humor), this type of dual-purpose social act may be fragmented into its underlying constituents, as in the following rather typical interchange between a mother and her son (32 months) as they look at the pictures in a favorite story book:

Mother	Jack
You see what this little boy is doing? (*Points at a picture.*)	
	Yeah.
What's he doing?	
	He's chasing this rabbit.
He's chasing the rabbit away.	

Jack's failure to volunteer the information about what he sees (whatever the reason for this failure) leads to his mother's reformulating the question directly. (The mother indicates that her second question is in some way a *re*formulation by emphasizing the question word *what* rather than the final word, *doing.*) Whether the purpose of her initial formulation was to direct Jack's attention, as the literal reading would suggest, or to solicit a response specifying what the little boy was doing, as an indirect interpretation might suggest, we cannot say with certainty. What we can say, however, is that the particular shape of this task was influenced by *both* participants, by what both actually said and did, by each person's expectations and beliefs about the other person and each one's current state of knowledge and attention, and by their understanding of the nature of the talk engagement. In all but a few special cases, which we shall discuss in Chapter 7, text is a product of collaborative effort at each moment of its production.

STUDYING TALK

We are so surrounded by talk that most of us pay little attention to it directly and are interested only in its effects. In order to think about talk or talk about it, we must become conscious of it as a phenomenon in its own right. For this task we need to understand certain terms and concepts, some of which will be introduced in this chapter.

Talk is a very complex activity. Like other human activities, it unfolds in time. It happens and disappears very rapidly, leaving only a suggestive trace in memory. When we capture it by recordings, in writing, or more completely in audio or video records, we have a more faithful reproduction of it, although the rehearing is a very different experience from either hearing it or taking part in it as it took place. The analyst can examine a record of talk at leisure and can study the outcome to help interpret what preceded. Participants and overhearers must often suspend or revise a judgment as talk progresses, sometimes reinterpreting what transpired in light of a finally revealed objective. A participant hears what is happening somewhat differently from an analyst or observer because his motive is different; he listens in order to respond appropriately, in order to decide what to do and say next.

What the analyst examines in retrospect is an object rather than the action itself. To understand it, the analyst must assign the recorded tokens to analytical or interpretive categories, or types, at various levels of organization. For example, one piece of talk might for different purposes be classified as a noun, a label, the subject of a sentence, a topic, or a referring expression; another piece as an utterance, a sentence type, a statement, a turn-at-speaking, an answer, a response, or a challenge. As might be expected in any new field of study, investigators, who may have quite different objectives for their work, often differ among themselves as to the categories and even as to the levels of structure they postulate and in the procedures for the assignment of tokens to those types. They may also approximate the interpretations of the actual producers of the talk to a greater or lesser degree.

When the producers of talk are young children, the investigators' analytical schemes may diverge considerably from the producers' point of view. Children have not yet learned to read and write and are unable to segment talk into words and grammatical structures, to view talk as an object rather than as a part of their own and others' actions, or to classify tokens of talk into types. They will only gradually learn how to distinguish the act of talking from the resultant linguistic object tokens and acquire the techniques and vocabulary for talking about types and for distinguishing the various levels of the organization of talk. And although they will eventually acquire such metalinguistic and metacommunicative skills, they will, like most adults, attend to only some aspects of the workings of language and talk and only when something is perceived to be wrong in either comprehension or production. Under normal circumstances talk is transparent; speakers manipulate meanings for their own purposes but do not see the various levels of structure that make it possible to formulate those meanings.

The situation. Talk is always situated, and to a large extent it derives its significance from the situation. It occurs somewhere, at some time, among certain people (or perhaps from a solitary person) engaged in doing something or several things. Talking is the most common means of conducting a social event, be it a trial, a rap session, a lesson, a welcome-home party. Talk is highly sensitive to its context and to the purposes it serves in an event, and it covaries with them in form and function. This fact creates two problems for the investigator of talk and of social activity. First, recorded talk is necessarily removed from the situation that motivated and influenced it in the first place, making it difficult to determine the factors that influenced this chameleonlike phenomenon. Second, there is no way to remove situational influence from talk, although certainly the situational factors can be varied and manipulated. An investigator can control, for example, the number, sex, age, and relationship of the persons; can record talk in the home, at school, on the playground; or can ask the participants to talk for some particular purpose, such as solving a problem cooperatively, instructing a partner in how to do something, or even pretending to argue. But the investigator cannot create a situation in which talk does not subtly adapt itself to what the talkers conceive to be the purpose of the engagement and to what they see as the relevant features of the situation. Sociolinguists accept these facts about talk as their primary concern. They study the covariation of talk and the socially defined features of situations, and they usually prefer to make their observations under relatively natural conditions, allowing those naturally occurring changes in the situation to furnish the variation in situational factors.

Another aspect of the situatedness of talk, however, is the fact that talkers are continuously interpreting what is going on and what they are doing, and they adjust their talk to that interpretation. This can occur even in the most rigorously controlled observation situation. Similarly, if people are given tokens of talk to interpret in an experimental task, they will usually construct a context for the orphaned sentences or utterances in order to make sense of them; different people may construct very different contexts within which to make their interpretations. This distinctly human process of interpreting, that is, of creating at least in part the very situation to which one then reacts, is itself of interest and is the central topic of investigation of ethnomethodologists. These analysts of talk search for the ways in which people try to make sense of ongoing interactions and how they jointly construct, or interpret, their purposes and the social-psychological context of their activity.

Units of talk. In any piece of talk, many things may be going on at once. The information presented, the illocutionary force intended and perceived, the meanings implied or inferred can be "packaged," or encoded, in alternative ways, using different linguistic devices, and can be distributed among the speakers and over time in different ways. Further, the import of a given piece of talk depends to a considerable extent on exactly where that piece occurs in relation to what has preceded it and what may follow, as was illustrated in the prior example containing the *re*formulation. These facts about the nature of talk contribute to the difficulty of defining and identifying its units, abstract concepts that can be instantiated by the actual variable tokens of talk. The units must be defined in such a way as to accommodate the accordianlike versatility of talk. Any description or analysis requires units that can be identified and counted by different people with a reasonable degree of consensus. This objective can be achieved for talk only by distinguishing the several aspects of organization in any instance of talking and then postulating unit types that are appropriate for describing talk from these different perspectives.

Although the linguistic clause is the basic unit for analyzing the choices speakers can make from the perspective of the grammar and lexicon of their language, it is not the basic unit for the physical production of speech. That basic unit is the phonological clause, or tone unit,[9] each of which has one loudest, or most prominent, syllable. Thus, a speaker can produce one linguistic clause in one tone unit or in two or more, depending on his phrasing and emphasis. From the perspective of the distribution of talk among speakers, the basic unit is the turn-at-speaking, the unit that captures the dynamic processes of the exchange of rights and obligations to speak. A turn-at-speaking can contain one or more linguistic clauses and one or more tone units.

The units and the perspective for which they are appropriate are described below.

The smallest units of talk:

Tone group: a unit of linguistic organization from the perspective of its intonational, or prosodic, structure.

Clause: a unit of linguistic organization from the perspective of its lexicogrammatical structure.

Utterance: a neutral term that refers to the extent of one person's speech. An utterance is sometimes defined as one person's speech bounded by pauses or by the speech of another person. It usually ends with an intonation pattern that indicates the speaker has stopped talking—a terminal intonation contour.

Turn, or *turn-at-speaking:* a unit of the distribution among the different speakers of the right or obligation to talk in a talk engagement.

Move: a unit of meaningful social action within an identifiable procedure or activity. Rather like a move in a game, moves in talk are sequenced and distributed among the speakers' social roles in an encounter or engagement.

Speech act: a unit of meaningful social and linguistic action. It refers to what the speaker is doing. Unlike *move,* this term does not imply a procedure, and unlike *turn* it does not imply a talk exchange.

Message: a neutral term that refers to what is meant and said from the perspective of content, but unlike the term *speech act* it does not imply the possibility of classification as a particular type of speech act.

I also use the term *proposition* in this book, although it is not a unit of talk. It is, rather, an abstract unit of logical or semantic structure. A proposition, *The cat is gray,* which relates the two concepts, *the cat* and *gray,* can be judged true or false.

Larger units of talk:

Exchange: two linked units, usually contiguous, one from each of two speakers. Although the units in an exchange are linked, the term does not imply the nature of the link.

Sequence: two or more minimal units, provided by one or more speakers, that have a particular function in talk, for example, a repair sequence (see Chapter 2) embedded in an exchange or episode.

Interchange: a neutral term that refers to a piece of talk produced by two or more speakers.

Episode: a unit, comprising three or more linked exchanges, usually characterized by some thematic continuity or organization and usually with no change of participants or social roles.

Talk engagement, encounter, or *speech event:* These terms, which refer to the whole of an event, differ only minimally. A talk engagement does not imply any particular kind of activity or procedure. An encounter implies some sort of objective, such as making a purchase, and its form is shaped by the objective. A speech event implies a particular type of engagement in which place, time, participants, and objectives are conventionally organized, such as a lecture, a job interview, or a classroom lesson.

I do not guarantee that I use these terms in exactly the same way as other authors cited in the references, although the above descriptions have attempted to capture some consensus in usage.

THE STUDY OF CHILDREN'S TALK

Despite the recent enthusiasm for recording, describing, and analyzing children's talk, the sampling has been restricted to a few situations. The primary ones are the nursery school or day care center, where talk with both peers and teachers has been observed; the home, where the focus has been talk with the mother in relaxed play or, more rarely, in the press of everyday activities; and more controlled situations, either in a laboratory or at home, where the child is observed performing some set task in interaction with either the mother or an investigator. Only in the last few years have investigators attempted to record talk with fathers or siblings or the child's talk when alone. Children's talk with pets, baby sitters, relatives, family friends, strangers, doctors, and nurses has rarely, if ever, been examined. And only in a few instances has the same child's talk been compared in different situations or with different partners. Usually, too, a child is recorded only once or twice in the same situation; relatively few studies have attempted to follow the same children over a longer period of time after they have acquired the fundamentals of language. The sampling of the functional differentiation and elaboration of talk during the preschool years is thus less than complete.

As to diversity of the children's and families' cultural and linguistic backgrounds, here, too, the records are less than representative. Language socialization, the role played by talk in the child's induction into the social world of his family and group, may differ considerably across cultures and even between English-speaking communities in close geographical proximity.[10] The cultural group may determine whether and when, for example, a four-year-old is permitted, encouraged, or forbidden to ask questions of adults, and, if permitted, whether he may ask about matters of fact or of the imagination.[11] At this time, therefore, any claims about the uses and nature of children's talk must be hedged about with disclaimers, and one should specify the sources of the observations on which the claims rest.

In this book I have made extensive use of observations by other investigators, most of which are cited in the reference section. In many cases I have illustrated other investigators' findings with examples from my own recordings. Happily, the talk of the children I have recorded is very similar to the talk observed by many others because of the similarity of the populations. When a child's linguistic or cultural background differs from those of the children described below, this is noted in the text.

The children studied. My source of data and observations is a collection of video and audio recordings made over a period of approximately ten years. There are two groups of recordings. The children in the first group, identified in the text as the three- to five-year-olds or children in the laboratory playroom, were contacted through local nursery schools that served a predominantly white, middle-class community. The children ranged in age from 34 months to 67 months. Nursery school teachers were asked to bring three children from the same classroom, who were familiar with each other, to a playroom at the university. Each group of three contained two children of the same sex. There were four groups of the youngest children, four groups between the ages of 42 and 52 months, and eight groups of the oldest children; in all, forty-eight children, twenty-one boys and twenty-seven girls. When the children arrived at the playroom, two of the three were allowed to enter the playroom and play with anything they liked; the third child was busied with some games in another room. The teacher accompanied the investigators into an observation room, where the children's activity and talk was recorded. No adults were present in the playroom. At the end of fifteen minutes, the pair of children was changed, so that in all, each child was observed twice, with two different partners, for a total of thirty minutes. Another sixty children were observed in a similar manner, but these children were not previously acquainted and were drawn from both day care centers and nursery schools. The age range of this group was 36 months to 48 months. Each child in this group was observed only once along with a child of the same sex.[12]

The playroom was furnished with a rug, a couch, some pictures on the wall, a small table, and chairs. In the middle of the room, directly under a microphone concealed by a stuffed parrot, was a rectangular wooden "car," just large enough for two children to sit on. It had painted wheels, a real license plate, and a real steering wheel that could turn. Other toys included stuffed animals, a toy stove with pans, dishes, and eating utensils, two baby dolls and a little cradle, an ironing board and iron, a set of toy carpenter's tools, two ladies' handbags with some jewelry inside, a suitcase and a box containing dress-up clothes, several puzzles, books and pencils, little cars, trucks, and some blocks.

The second group of recordings was made for a short longitudinal study of forms of talk among somewhat younger children. Sarah, Judy, and Jack were recorded under different conditions for five months; they were 25 months, 28 months, and 30 months, respectively, at the time of the first video recording at home. Each child's "best friend" (identified by the mother as the peer with whom the child spent the most time) was included in the study: Sarah's friend Becky (34 months), Judy's friend Tom (29 months), and Jack's friend Anne (31 months). All the children were from white, middle-class families. The fathers were associated with the university as graduate students or staff, the mothers with one exception were not employed outside the home, and all the children but Becky were only children at the beginning of the recordings. Video recordings approximately thirty minutes long were made each month in the home of each child with best friend and of child with mother during their usual play times. Each pair of children also came to the laboratory playroom once a month, where they were video recorded alone for approximately one hour, the mothers remaining on call in the observation room. Since the children had already had experience in a co-op play group where their mothers left them for an hour or two, they accepted the separation from their mothers in the playroom without protest. Additionally, each of the three mothers made audio recordings each month of herself engaged in a household task or in routine activity with the child and of the child alone, either at bedtime or nap time, or when the child was engaged in a solitary monologue.

Talk assumes ever-increasing importance in the child's life from the first verbal exchanges with caregivers, which begin to appear before the second birthday, through the preschool period. With the beginning of formal education, new people and new experiences create the need for other uses of talk. Perhaps the most dramatic changes and the most impressive achievements occur during the third year of life. The child is well on his way toward learning language, has a vocabulary of about five hundred words, and is well aware that talk serves vital functions in both social and private life. Edward Mueller and his colleagues found that among three boys in a play group, between the ages of 22 and 30 months the mean percentage of the utterances that received a verbal response from a partner increased from 27 percent to 64 percent. Since prior listener attention was the strongest predictor of which utterances would receive a response, it is likely that the children were learning something about the interpersonal contingencies of talking[13] even when the partner was a peer. Among the youngest peers (34–39 months) in our playroom observations, talk generally accompanied almost everything they did; the pairs produced, on the average, one utterance every six seconds, and both members contributed in rather similar degrees to the talk. (For the older pairs, talk was even more frequent and even more likely to be equitably distributed between the members.) Talk, I believe, is central to most aspects of the child's life, and the early period at which the child himself is becoming aware of the importance of talk is one of the most exciting in the annals of the developing child.

Limitations. The sampling of children's talk remains extremely limited both in respect to cultural and geographic diversity and in respect to the situations in which it occurs and the purposes it can serve. Even within the groups and families of the children who have been studied, reports do not fairly capture the range of differences that probably exist in this immensely rich and diversified human activity. Other limitations in my coverage of this broad and complex topic result from the emphasis of the book itself, which is limited to the preschool period. Even for this period I have omitted certain topics, for example, the development of narrative skills and other aspects of talk as an art form, such as jokes and riddles. Also neglected here is the talk of children who for various reasons do not proceed along the normal course of development. Blindness, deafness, physical or social deprivation, and other kinds of illness and handicap can impede or distort the growth of talk in various ways, many of which are as yet poorly understood. Children's means of compensating for these impediments to full communicative activity will be an important topic for future study.

A boy (50 months) and a girl, Melissa (52 months), from the same nursery school class talk in a laboratory playroom. (See page 33 for an explanation of the arrows.)

Boy	Girl
Lisa is your nickname.	
	What? ↗
You're/ you/ you want to know your nickname?	
	What? ↘
Lisa.	
	No. *Me*lissa.
Melissa?	
	Yeah, Melissa.
Well, Lisa, Melissa. Well, Lisa, teacher calls you Lisa.	
	What? ↗
Teacher calls you *Lisa*.	
	I know that, but that isn't my nickname. (*Pause.*) How long before our friends come back?
Who? ↘	
(*No response. He watches her a second and turns away.*)	The lady who was here a minute ago. (*Looks in the one-way mirror and makes faces at herself.*)

2 / The Transmission System

Talking with another person requires the simultaneous engagement of several interconnected systems—a transmission system, a tracking and guidance system, and what might be called a facilitation system. The first system operates to assure the sending and reception of messages, the second to identify meanings, and the third to assure that the messages are acceptable and appropriate to the participants. To continue the mechanical metaphor, many kinds of talk also require a fuel system, the motive force for talk, which includes meanings, intentions, and actions to be communicated. These systems have been variously named, and their components have been assigned to different systems; such difficulties reflect both the complexity of talking and the fact that the systems and their components are interdependent. Only some components of each system have been studied in adult talk, and even fewer have been examined from a developmental perspective. But even what is known at this time forcibly reveals just how complex an activity talk is and how much the young child must eventually learn in order to participate in social talk as an equal partner. In this chapter I will discuss the requirements of the first system and how children begin to cope with them.

31

The transmission system deals with speaker contact and the ordering and distribution of the speakers' activity. First, the speaker must be assured of the addressee's attention and availability. Thereafter, the onset and closing of talk engagements are marked, as are the boundaries of any specialized units of talk that may be embedded in a talk engagement, for example, a narrative within a conversation. If special interpretative procedures are called for, as when the speaker is quoting the speech of another person, these must be flagged for the addressee. During a talk engagement the participants exchange signals that the transmission is successful and that mutual attention is being maintained. If a problem arises in reception or understanding, a repair must be made as soon as the flaw is detected. Perhaps the most important task of the transmission system is to assure that turns-at-speaking are exchanged and, especially in multiparty engagements, allocated smoothly and efficiently. In this system some scholars have also included the fundamental rules of the speaker's (or actor's) responsibility: the speaker is expected to say what he believes is true, what is relevant to the task at hand, and no more, and to do so as clearly as possible. These demands are met primarily through verbal and vocal means, as is clear from telephone conversations or talk between two different rooms; but in face-to-face engagements, gestures, physical attitudes, and spatial orientation complement or replace some parts of the verbal or vocal work. We can now examine the operation of some components of the transmission system in more detail.

ATTENTION AND AVAILABILITY

Even very young children recognize the need to open up the communication channel, although they may not recognize the need to close it. The preverbal child has learned to engage an adult's attention by seeking eye contact and by using gesture and vocalization. The child just learning to talk will often use a vocative: "Mommy!" or vocative plus attention-getting word: "Mommy. Look!" If the initial vocative fails to get the desired result, the child usually repeats it in a second or two, possibly several times. A response such as "Yes, dear!" or even "Hm?" is the clearance signal for the child to continue. When two- or three-year-olds initiate an engagement with a bare message, as sometimes happens when they approach strangers and offer them a topic ("I'm three today" or "This is my doll"), it is a bit disconcerting just because they have omitted a prior move designed to assure addressee availability. Children of three or four years add other techniques for opening up the channel of communication; a favorite is the question, "Know what?↗" It leads the addressee to an involuntary return question, "What?↘" and the initiator has a clear invitation to say what he wanted to say in the first place. (An arrow pointing upward indicates a rising pitch at the end of an utterance. An arrow pointing downward indicates a falling pitch. When placed after the question mark, the arrow signals that the written form is ambiguous. "What?" can be uttered with either a rising or a falling pitch, and "What?↗" has, in context, a different meaning from "What?↘". The upward arrow is also used to emphasize rising pitch in a particular utterance.)

Because of the distractibility of very young children and the desire of adults to engage them in talk, adults give children frequent attention-getting signals. When trying to talk with two-year-olds, slightly older children similarly use a high proportion of such signals. Nursery school children who are already available to one another, sharing a play space and a common activity, like familiar adults, often assume that the partner's attention can be retrieved. In the condition that Erving Goffman has called "an open state of talk,"[1] clearance signals are not required, and partners are expected to be at least within one another's peripheral attention at all times. Talk may alternate between being an accompaniment to some other activity and being the primary focus for both partners, and it may alternate between private talk for self and talk that is clearly directed to the partner in expectation of a response. When two or three young peers are together at work or play, this is the most common state of engagement. As I discuss below, this affects the operation of the turn-taking component as well. The task of gaining the attention and securing the availability of others becomes most challenging and problematic in such situations as competing for the limited individual attention of a busy nursery school teacher or achieving access to a group of peers who are already engaged in some activity. I describe how children deal with the access problem in Chapter 6.

Seeking the availability of a teacher and assuring one's right to her attention and reply often call for persistence and ingenuity. The sometimes valiant efforts made by children in classrooms from nursery through third grade to secure a clearance signal from their teachers have been examined by Marilyn Merritt.[2] She videotaped sessions of individualized instruction in which the teacher, busy with one child or with several in a group activity, was solicited by another. The solicitor's ultimate objective was either to submit a topic outside the teacher's activity field or to raise an individual problem that might or might not be related to what the teacher and children were doing. In one instance a kindergarten child addressed a comment to the teacher who had been working with her, but the teacher had already turned her attention to another child. The solicitor repeated her comment but this time prefaced it with a vocative. She repeated this ploy twice and still failed to get the teacher's attention; then she reverted to the vocative alone, using the rising intonation that is designed to induce the teacher to reply with a clearance signal: "What?↗" or "Yes?↗" She repeated this strategy twice and failed, then made eight more attempts, using the previous techniques. Finally the teacher, finished with her work with the other child, responded.

MARKING BOUNDARIES AND PROGRESS

Speakers need to know where they are in a talk engagement in order to know what to do next. Telephone conversations, which are among the most highly structured of informal engagements, provide a paradigm.[3] Initial hellos are exchanged, functioning to clear the channel, then further greetings, "How are you?" before the purported topic or reason for the call can be raised. After the topic has been discussed, adults begin to "open up" the closing portion of the call, thus giving each speaker the opportunity to raise additional topics. If neither wishes to do so (signaled by one or more exchanges of "Well"—"Well, okay"), the conversation is terminated with an exchange of goodbyes, and perhaps a ritual fillip such as "See you"—"Yeah." (A dash between quotations indicates a change of speaker.) Children grasp the structure of a telephone call as a nicely delimited event, though, of course, at first they have as a model only one speaker's contribution. Interestingly, they appear to learn the outer boundary markers first. The earliest reproduction of telephoning in pretend play (and sometimes in real life if an adult fails to intervene when a two-year-old answers the telephone at home) is "Hello. Goodbye." In the next stage the child supplies the greetings: "Hello. How are you? Fine. Goodbye." The next stage may elaborate these moves and add a hint of a substantive topic: "Hello. How are you? I'm fine. I'm ironing. Goodbye." At this level of sophistication the child begins to leave pauses for the replies of the pretend interlocutor and to use a vacant stare into space, the "telephone gaze." By four years of age a pretend conversation with an imaginary or actual partner is likely to have more topic talk and occasionally a preclosing move: "Well, I have to go now. I have to do some work for the baby," before the final round of goodbyes.

Within an engagement also participants need to know if some special form of talk has been instituted and when that special segment ends. Thus if a personal narrative, a sequence of instructions, or a joke is introduced, its boundaries are also signaled. Such special forms require suspending the regular rules for alternating turns-at-speaking and often require the addressee to use appropriately timed signals of continuing attention and satisfactory reception, which are called *back-channel feedback*. While preschoolers know the traditional boundary markers for stories and use them when asked to tell a story, they are less skilled at packaging and inserting personal narratives into ongoing conversations. The first step acquired in learning to package a narrative or story, however, is marking its onset, usually by distinguishing the time of the reported or recounted event from the present time by a time marker such as *once, one time,* or *yesterday.*

BACK-CHANNEL FEEDBACK

These are the head nods, the *um-huh*'s, the *hmm*'s that addressees send to speakers during lengthy turns-at-speaking, at the rate of about one every five to seven seconds in an adult engagement. They are a relatively late development in children's interactive talk. Perhaps young children do not realize that a speaker needs feedback. Or perhaps children have few opportunities to use this kind of feedback because adults direct short turns-at-speaking to them while explicitly requesting their response. When adults do take longer turns, as in telling or reading a story, they frequently check on the child's continued attention and understanding with probes such as "Then what happened?" or by asking the child to point to a picture or referent object or to complete a line of the story or poem. Because back-channel signals are intimately related to the turn-taking component and must be inserted very precisely into the partner's ongoing messages with regard not only to meaning but also to timing, it is not surprising that their use is well developed only toward adolescence.

REPAIRS

Talk exchanges are subject to mishearings, misfire, mistakes, and flaws at every level of construction. A repair must be made as soon as the mistake is detected, sometimes even before it fully happens, as it is caught in midstream or anticipated. In adult talk there is a decided preference for *self-initiated repairs* in production—a fix-it-yourself policy—before the partner notices or intervenes.[4] The preference implies constant self-monitoring of one's own speech and plans for speech as well as continuous monitoring of the partner's probable detection or interpretation of the emerging message. Performing a repair on a partner's message, or simply calling attention to a flaw in his transmission or in one's understanding, is called *other-initiated repair* and also requires continuous monitoring. The task ranges in difficulty from simply realizing that the partner has spoken and that one failed to hear what was said, in which case "Huh?" or "I beg your pardon?" usually suffices to elicit a replay of the message, to cases in which one compares a well-received message with the anticipated message, notes the difference, and searches for the cause of the discrepancy. Figuring out whether the problem is in the partner's production or in one's own understanding may require more complex mental processing. Adults have an array of techniques for repairing particular kinds of flaws: "I thought you meant to say—"; "He did *what*?"; "I missed the first part of that." Even in other-initiated repairs, the preference seems to be to allow the speaker to make the necessary correction if he is responsible for the flaw. Thus norms for conversational conduct, cognitive processing demands, and linguistic techniques for pointing out and correcting problems are all involved in the repair component.

We will first examine self-initiated repairs. Young children have production problems that seem to be exacerbated when they attempt to produce complex messages. For example, Tom (32 months) tried to answer Judy's question as to why his tummy was hurting the other day: " 'Cause i-/i-/i-/i-/i-/ it was hurting cause i-/ it was hurting because it was hurting/ . . . and/ . . . and it feels all better now." (A slash indicates an abrupt termination of speech, a self-interruption. Ellipsis dots within an utterance indicate a brief pause or hesitation; at the end of an utterance they indicate that the speaker has stopped or faded out before completing the utterance.) He stuttered, starting words without finishing them, he repeated words and phrases, retracing over the false start, and there were brief periods of silence (unfilled pauses) in his speech. His production problems were not marked by filled pauses, which are points of hesitation occupied by the little noises written as *"um," "er,"* or *"uh,"* though some children of Tom's age do use these distress signals. In the speech of preschoolers filled and unfilled pauses and retracings with corrections are common. Preschoolers do not yet, however, differentiate the more precise signals that adults use to suggest the type of encoding problem they are encountering. For adults, the interjections "oh," "ah," "well," and "say" have specialized meanings. For example, "I think I'll have—oh—scallops" suggests that the speaker has considered other alternatives; but "I think I'll have—ah—scallops" indicates that he had temporarily forgotten the name of the dish he wanted.[5] Nor do children begin to use the self-correction phrases—"that is," "rather," "I mean"—that adults use for immediate revision of the content of prior speech until about six years of age. Adult speakers put considerable effort into "getting it right," in part because a flaw may lead a partner to intervene with a correction or request for repair. Filled pauses and retracings indicate to a partner that the current speaker intends to continue. Four- and five-year-olds are beginning to learn that in talk he who hesitates is lost; fillers such as "y'know" and other devices can often fend off an impatient partner until the speaker concludes his turn. This function of the repair devices is discussed below.

Other-initiated repairs either provide a correction or invite the speaker to furnish one himself. In either case, the repair work is attended to immediately and takes precedence over any other concerns. However, flaws in production or reception are not always detected. Parents often ask children to repeat a message so flawed that it cannot be understood, but in general parents are notoriously lax in calling attention to errors in children's pronunciation and grammar; they are more apt to pursue repairs concerning word meanings, matters of fact, and politeness and other conversational protocol.

The dominant goal of other-initiated repair is to elicit some type of clarification. The primary means are requests, usually in question form. Often called *clarification requests*, these moves invite the speaker to make a repair, the nature of which is more or less directly indicated by the question. If the repair is made satisfactorily, the flow of talk will continue; if the repair is not made, the invitation to repair will be repeated or replaced by an outright correction. Repairs, then, are best studied as sequences within the flow of conversation. In describing repair sequences, we call the message that is the occasion for the repair work M0; the repair invitation or correction is M1; and the replayed or repaired message responding to M1 is M2. If the sequence is successful, the next message can resume the conversation or otherwise continue the interaction, perhaps introducing a new topic; if it is unsuccessful, the repair sequence is recycled. A repair sequence often makes up an entire conversational episode in the talk of young children. The following example illustrates a recycled repair using several common repair moves.

Judy (32 months) and Tom (33 months) are having a tea party. Judy has just taken charge of the bag of raisins:

Tom	Judy	Comments
M0: I want three.		
	M1: Huh?↗	Nonspecific request for repetition.
M2: I want three.		Replay of M0 as requested.
	M1: Hum?↗	Second nonspecific request for repetition

M0: (Prior M2 now functions as a new M0.)

M2: I want three.

M1: Three? ↗

M0: (Prior M2 now functions as a new M0.)

M2: Yeah.

turns the replayed M2 into another M0, a message in need of repair.

Replayed again. Specific request for confirmation, turns replayed M2 into M0.

Tom confirms Judy's request as correct.

Judy now needs more information in order to comply with Tom's thoroughly clarified request which, as it is not actually uttered again, I indicate in brackets.

M0: [I want three.]

M1: Where? ↘

Request for elaboration.

M2: On my plate.

Supplies the added information, but becomes in turn a new occasion for repair.

M0: (Prior M2 now functions as a new M0.)

M1: Oh, right there? ↗

Specific request for confirmation.

M2: Yep.

Tom confirms Judy's formulation as correct.

I like my . . . (fades out).

Whether Tom faded out because of his interest in the raisins Judy finally placed on his plate or from sheer exhaustion, we don't know, but with Judy's cooperation, the message, which cumulatively conveyed the information, "I want three [raisins] here on my plate," was ultimately transmitted. Judy's questions, each of which was contingent on Tom's prior moves, selected different aspects of what Tom had said (or failed to say in the case of her question, "Where?") and at the same time indicated to him just what type of answer would meet her needs at that point in the exchange. She was monitoring her own needs for understanding rather precisely in order, we presume, to carry out appropriate action. Actually, even at this age children command still other types of repair moves beyond those illustrated above.

The basic moves that preschoolers and adults use can be described as follows. The means for selecting the flaw or inadequacy in the M0 may be nonspecific, with no specific element of the M0 pinpointed; specific, with some component selected; or potential, with some component selected that is potentially relevant to the M0 but that has not been previously encoded. Judy's "Hum?" is an example of the nonspecific; "What?↗" and "I beg your pardon?" are alternatives. Judy's questions, "Three?↗" and "Oh, right there?↗" are examples of specific elements selected from the M0. Her question "Where?↘" is an example of a potential selection; Tom's message had not indicated a location, but such information could have been encoded in the message. Potential selections are not strictly speaking repair work of an issued message, but they can provide the partner with information necessary for full understanding of that message.

In addition to selecting from the M0, the repair move indicates to the partner just what kind of repair is desired. There are four broad categories: repetition or replay, specification, confirmation, and elaboration. Judy's "Hum?" asked for repetition; her "Three?↗" and "Oh, right there?↗" suggested a repair and asked for confirmation of its acceptability. Her question, "Where?↘" asked for elaboration. If, after Tom replied, "On my plate," she had asked, "Which plate?↘" she would have been requesting specification, and Tom's cooperative response might have been "The blue one" if he had more than one plate.

The means for selecting the matter for repair and the means of indicating the kind of response needed, taken together, provide a number of move types that permit very precise repair work. The type of move intended, however, is often indicated solely by the intonation. If Tom had said, "I need something on my plate," Judy might have asked, "What?↗" or "What?↘" In the first case, which is a nonspecific request for repetition, Tom would probably have repeated his whole utterance; in the second case, which is a specific request for specification (of the indefinite pronoun), he would have replied, "Raisins." The example is not a hypothetical one: intonation alone disambiguates a number of otherwise identical repair moves, and by the age of three most children both respond to and issue such minimally different clarification requests spontaneously.[6] Further examples of the move types common in child–child and child–adult talk will be provided as we discuss how this system of other-initiated repair is acquired and used.

As young children begin to talk, adults very frequently respond to their messages with return, or feedback, questions. Many of these are requests for clarification, though even these may also have a goal of encouraging and extending conversational interchange. (Moves with a single interactional function are rare regardless of the age of the interlocutors.) Of course, adults can initiate repairs on a child's message in noninterrogative form, but they often prefer to appear, at least, to give the child some opportunity to either repair or accept the repair. To do the latter, adults append a tag question to what would otherwise be a bare assertion of the correct form. For example, a child of 21 months incorrectly answered his mother's question about a shape: M: "What does that look like?" C: "A eight." M: "It looks like a square, doesn't it?" The child accepted the correction and repeated the identification, saying, "Square."

In a study of repair work in talk between adults and young children, Tanya Gallagher recorded the speech of an adult with children at three levels of linguistic development, the children ranging in age from 22 to 36 months.[7] The adult issued requests for clarification at an average rate of one every three minutes. The most common type was the request for confirmation. Less frequent were nonspecific requests for repetition and specific requests for repetition of a constituent of the child's message. The latter type has been called an *occasional question:* it replaces a constituent with a *wh* question word: C: "I want some juice." A: "You want some *what?*↗" or "Some *what?*↗" The children varied in their ability to respond differentially to these types of invitations to repair. All the children responded appropriately to invitations to confirm. They showed a decided preference for affirmative responses, even in a few cases where a negative one would have been correct. To nonspecific requests for repetition, children repeated or revised what they had said before. (Revision is an acceptable response to this type of request, even among adult conversationalists.) Only the children who were more advanced in linguistic development replied to the occasional questions with just the specified constituent; the others generally responded with repetition or revision, or not at all. The children initiated repairs on the adult's speech less frequently than the adult requested repair. This is a common finding in experimental or nursery school settings, even among children as old as six or seven years, and reflects, most likely, the difference in status rather than linguistic skill alone. Requests for confirmation by the children were more frequent than nonspecific requests for repetition. The occasional question was used rarely and by only three of the children.

When we examined all the questions that Sarah, Judy, and Jack addressed to the just-prior speech of their best friends and of their mothers over the five-month period of the study, we found that repair requests constituted from 40 to 65 percent of those questions, with somewhat more directed to the peer partner than to the mother. Less than one third of each child's repair questions were nonspecific requests for repetition with a slightly higher proportion of "huh?"'s directed to the peer partner than to the mother. Thus these very young children had no qualms about asking their mothers for clarification, but either they attended more carefully to their mothers' speech or, more often, they found that their friends' speech required repetition.

The basic course of development of repair capabilities can be summarized as follows. Well before the age of two, children begin to respond to other-initiated repairs. These repairs are simple ones at first, requesting only confirmation or repetition, and children attempt to provide the appropriate repair response (although occasionally they simply do not answer). As children's linguistic skill increases, adults begin to issue queries requesting specific feedback, and children answer them. Between the ages of three and four, children can issue a variety of repair requests, even those that pinpoint a specific constituent in the flawed message, and they begin to request relevant information that is not in the prior message. The repair sequences are, by this age, neatly embedded in the flow of conversation, as the following example illustrates:

Girl (42 months)	*Boy (43 months)*
M0: But . . . uh . . . driver man. I have to drive this car.	
	M1: What car? ↘
	M1: This car? ↗ (*Touches wooden car he is sitting on.*)
M2: Yes.	
	I . . . can't/ You can't. I'm the dad.

The boy issued a specific request for specification, then, in a self-initiated repair, rephrased it to a specific request for confirmation. That received an immediate response, and the boy then responded to the girl's now clarified message, although he himself encountered a production problem and had to retrace his speech in a self-initiated repair, changing "I . . . can't" to "You can't." The pattern of modification from a request for specification (the first M1), presumably more difficult for the partner to answer, to a request for confirmation (the second M1) is a familiar pattern in the speech of adults to children as well and is used when the child fails to respond or responds incorrectly.

Throughout this course of development the child learns to detect an increasing number of aspects of a prior message as requiring repair, by means of either clarification questions or outright assertions of correction. In peer interactions during the preschool years, children initiate repairs on the propositional content of messages, on the partner's manner of speaking (showing a partner, for example, how the partner in the role of Daddy should speak sternly to the Baby), on the choice of a particular word, and even on some other components of the transmission system. For example, Becky (36 months) who was talking to her doll, replied to Sarah's "Huh?" by saying, "I wasn't talking to you."

While the types of repair moves discussed above are both issued and responded to by three- and four-year-olds, the use of these or functionally comparable moves to repair one's own understanding or to assist the partner's understanding is still inconsistent and is dependent on the context and goal of talk. In the experimental setting of communication tasks, preschoolers often fail to question ambiguous information and also fail to frame their own messages to be maximally informative for the objective of the task. Feedback from a listener indicating just what type of correction or repair is needed generally improves their performance as speakers.[8] Knowing exactly what is missing or ambiguous in another's message involves not only scanning one's own knowledge state and the fit of the partner's message to the elements of the task, but also selecting just what one needs to elicit. Children's first requests for clarification arise, for the most part, in situations where they do not need to rely solely on the verbal channel. Thus, in the example above of the three-year-old boy and girl, the boy's pointing to the object complemented his verbally inadequate message. Learning to acquire needed information from the verbal channel alone by asking just the right question, as is required in most experimental communication tasks, is a difficult process that extends over the elementary school years. Interestingly, words themselves seem to trigger the process. Sarah at 26 months was already able to recognize that she did not know the meaning of a word in a familiar story, and she had the linguistic means for acquiring that specific information from her mother. Sarah sometimes requested definitions, which give the meaning of a word by using other words. In a typical example, Sarah was following the story of Cinderella as her mother read. Sarah pointed to one of the pictures and asked "Who's there?" Her mother replied, "That's one of the ladies of the land dressed in her beautiful best." Sarah, although she saw the picture, spotted a flaw in her own understanding and asked, "What's 'best'?" Her mother replied, "What's the best?↗ That's the very best dress she has."

TURN-TAKING

A fundamental requirement for conversation is the exchange of turns-at-speaking. Since the content and length of turns vary quite unpredictably, turn exchange cannot be accomplished automatically; the mechanism must be flexible. Ideally, the turn exchange is accomplished smoothly and rapidly, with one speaker relinquishing his turn and the next speaker beginning right away, neither overlapping the prior speaker's turn nor leaving any gap in the flow of talk. Harvey Sacks and his colleagues have described how this is accomplished in adult conversation.[9] Turns are constructed from linguistic units, that is, full clauses, major clause constituents, or their abridged equivalents. A turn may contain several such units, depending on what the speaker is doing in his talk, such as answering a question or describing a picture. Turns are exchanged at the boundary points of these units. Several mechanisms operate to effect a change of turn, and these are sequenced options. First, the current speaker can select the next speaker by passing the turn-at-speaking to that person, usually by asking a question, although in multiparty talk, the name of the selected next speaker is also used. Eye contact and other nonverbal techniques are also employed to signal turn transfer and to select next speaker. Second, if the current speaker does not select a next speaker, another person can select himself and assume his turn at a suitable boundary point. Third, if the current speaker does not select the next, and no next person initiates a turn, the current speaker may continue, selecting himself, in effect, as the next speaker.

Since turns-at-speaking are valued by the speakers, timing is of the essence. If a selected speaker does not immediately take the turn, the others may assume that he is not attending or is for some reason unable or unwilling to begin. If the current speaker has not selected the next speaker, anyone who wants to speak must begin quickly or risk having the current speaker resume *or* someone else take the next turn. Since the point at which a next speaker could begin is at the boundary of a turn construction unit, the potential next speaker must anticipate the upcoming boundary point. To do this, he must monitor the syntactic and semantic properties of the current speaker's message and type of move, so as to be ready to begin at just the right point. A minor miscalculation could lead to simultaneous talk, which is generally avoided, or to lapses in the flow of talk, which are generally discomforting for adults. Indeed, in focused engagements in which the primary activity is talk, the pauses, called switching pauses, between current and next speaker are extremely brief. They rarely exceed one second and are usually much shorter, averaging about one half second in adults' telephone conversations.[10]

This ideal system, of course, encounters operational

difficulties. Overlaps in turns do occur if two or more potential next speakers start talking at the same time, and often a current speaker is interrupted before he is ready to relinquish his turn. Repair mechanisms exist for these common problems. If two people begin a turn simultaneously, both may back off and try again. An interrupted current speaker generally overrides the interrupter by continuing to speak, perhaps at higher volume or pitch. Certain types of verbal social activity require simultaneous speech, such as chants, cheers, prayers, and other situations where the objective is expression of solidarity rather than exchange of ideas or attitudes. In conversation, however, the rule is one speaker's turn at a time.

Given the turn-transfer procedures and the repair techniques, there is little simultaneous talk in conversations, and what little does occur is very brief. Points of overlap occur primarily at the boundaries of turn construction units, where the current speaker goes on to add a next-speaker selection device. For example, the italicized portions of the following exchange overlap: A: "You could call him now, *couldn't you?*" B: "*Of course,* I could." A possible turn-exchange point followed the word *now;* the next speaker began precisely at that point, thereby accidentally overlapping the interrogative turn-transfer signal.

Turn-taking is sensitive to the speech situation, the relationships among the participants, and the goal of the talk engagement. Turn-taking in an interview, for example, has different rules from those for an informal chat. The inviolability of a current speaker's turn varies with that person's status. Adults interrupt children with relative impunity; men are more likely to interrupt women than the converse.[11]

The origins of conversational turn-taking probably lie

in the little games and playful conversations of caregivers with preverbal children. In the familiar game of peeka-boo, each person takes his appropriately sequenced turns, constituted of complementary actions. Timing varies in the exchange of turns, but there is a wait period or pause between the disappearance and reappearance of the object or person. Vocal markers accompany certain of the moves, and the surprise reappearance is usually greeted with oooh's and ah's. Over the period in which this game is popular, infants learn to take more and more responsibility for their own turns-at-acting.[12] But games are relatively rigid events, and the more likely precursors to conversational turn-taking are the early "conversations" themselves. Caregivers attempt to create conversations by allowing time for an infant to respond, or take a turn, and by treating any infant response as a turn, even a burp or chortle. In the absence of a response, the care-giver may reply for the infant or translate the burp or chortle into words. As children begin to talk, caregivers become more demanding and encourage the child to pro-duce his own verbal turns. This is one reason why there is such a high percentage of questions in the talk of care-givers. Children learn early on that questions require a response, and they sometimes begin to "answer" even before they are able to provide correct or appropriate re-plies. Mothers of children as old as three years continue to give the child assistance in taking and formulating a next turn. Questions continue to be important because they serve to pass the turn-at-speaking and also they guide the respondent in formulating the content and form of the response.

Before the age of three many children develop tech-niques for bypassing a proffered turn when they don't know what to say. Judy used "hmmm" to pass a turn back to her mother without making any real contribution herself. Sarah often simply repeated her mother's question word, thus passing the turn back, and Jack said "mmmm" to indicate that he recognized his turn obligation but had no other response available. How caregivers assist the child to take his turn is illustrated in the following example of Jack (30 months) and his mother reading a story about a baby bird.

Jack	Mother
	What is that called?
(No response.)	
	What is his home called?
	(Points at a picture of a nest.)
Mmmm.	
	Do you remember?
Mmmm.	
	Do we call a baby bird's home a nest?
Yeah!	
	That's right. It's a nest.

When Jack finally did formulate an acceptable response, with a lot of help from his mother, she expanded his reply as he might have done himself if he had been able. In this example Jack probably couldn't remember the needed word and thus issued his "I pass" signal. On other occasions he, and Judy as well, showed that they knew the speaking turn had been passed to them and that they intended to assume the turn as soon as possible. They used a marker to hold the turn: they would start by saying "uh," repeat it once or twice, and then provide their turn's talk. Adults also use this technique to signal, "I'm going to take my turn, but wait just a second." Both the "I pass" and the turn-holding signals indicate that children are aware of the obligation to take an offered turn and have learned what kind of move signals an obligatory turn transfer. Between the ages of two and three, they are also learning that the turn should be taken promptly.

TEMPORAL PATTERNS

Caregivers respond to a child's turn without delay, usually in less than one second, but children are not so prompt. But if their response is delayed beyond what the caregiver considers a normal response time, the caregiver urges them along by repeating or rephrasing the move. Caregivers notice the missing response and act to repair the failed turn transfer, usually within two seconds. The temporal patterning modeled by the caregiver becomes evident in the children's talk, even in exchanges between peers. Furthermore, the temporal patterning of conversation between peers is clearly differentiated from the patterns of social verbal play and from the more irregular patterns of acommunicative speech (talk not clearly directed to any person) early in the preschool period.

The best way to characterize the temporal patterning of conversation is to contrast it with that of a common type of social verbal play. Like conversation, ritualized play is made up of alternating turns-at-speaking, but the content, duration, and intonational pattern of the turns are relatively invariant within a ritualized play episode. In conversation the content is not predetermined, and the duration and intonation of each turn varies. The switching pause (SP) between speakers' turns is held almost constant during a particular ritual play episode, whereas in conversation the duration of the SPs varies within a restricted range. (Acommunicative speech, on the other hand, may be either repetitive or varied in content, but the duration of pauses may vary over a virtually unrestricted range; its timing is not constrained by the needs or actions of a partner.) The verbal ritual, then, is a rhythmic form of exchange, and each such event has its own temporal, intonational, and content patterning, more or less determined from the onset.[13] An excerpt from a longer episode will illustrate the patterning of one ritualized play produced by two three-year-olds. One child's turns consisted of saying, "No, I'm not"; the other child's consisted of "You are too." Each child's turn lasted between 0.5 and 0.9 seconds; the SPs varied between only 0.5 and 0.7 seconds. The intonation was the same with each repetition. In all, eleven turns were exchanged, all spoken in a rhythmic singsong manner. Unlike conversation, then, ritualized play permits automatic turn exchange, since the content is set and each child knows when the other is finished and what he himself will say next. But how do children deal with the more unpredictable rhythms of conversation?

In a study of the pauses in nonritualized talk among pairs of three- to five-year-olds, we examined all the exchanges in which a current speaker successfully transferred the turn to the next speaker, using a question or other turn-transfer technique.[14] We found that SP duration varied in exchanges but within a rather restricted range. Shorter SP durations were associated with simpler exchanges, such as a request for repetition and the repetition, or an exchange of greetings; longer SPs were associated with more complex exchanges, such as an episode initial *wh* question and response: "What's that noise?"— "Maybe it's a typewriter." The median SP duration for the simplest exchanges between three-year-olds was 0.9 seconds, and for the more complex exchanges it was 1.5

seconds. Among the older pairs the SP duration for the simplest exchanges was 0.7 seconds and for the more complex ones, 1.1 seconds. Within these types of exchanges, then, the children transferred turns promptly (though not as promptly as adults) and over the age range from three to five appeared to be narrowing the SP gap.

Not all turn-exchange offers are successful, however. We also examined those instances in which a child attempted to transfer the turn and failed. We found that the children noticed the missing response and reacted in much the same way that adults do under the same circumstances. After a pause they repeated or reformulated their unsuccessful move. What is most interesting is that when they did so, the pause before the replay move was longer than the median SP in more complex exchanges; the median duration of the notice-missing-response pause was 1.9 seconds for the three-year-olds and 2.0 seconds for the five-year-olds. These results suggest that children expect that a partner will assume the next turn, if invited to do so, and that if he is going to begin his turn, he will do so within the normal SP range. If the partner fails to take his turn, the speaker gives him a grace period of a little more than a half second and then tries again with another turn-transfer offer, attempting to repair the failure.

We also found, as have other observers, very few instances of simultaneous speech among pairs of peers. Among the younger children only 5 percent of the turns overlapped, and only 4 percent among the older children. Those instances that did occur were very brief, and the overlap rarely exceeded two words. The rarity of simultaneous speech, taken together with the data on switching pauses suggests that young children are aware of the one-turn-at-a-time rule for conversation. They are also aware that turns should be taken promptly and that a delay warrants or leads to repair work. Preschoolers, however, are not adept at the precision timing that adults exhibit. Rather than anticipating the upcoming boundary of the current speaker's turn, they are more likely to wait for cues that the current speaker has stopped before they begin a turn. Preschoolers are not uncomfortable with long lapses in talk. In semantically coherent conversational episodes SPs are brief, but in the play sessions as a whole, short periods of silence (20–40 seconds) were common, as might be expected in an open state of talk.

Young children's still fragile turn-taking skills are likely to be most effective in interchanges with one other person, which are, after all, their preferred and most frequent type of interaction. In multiparty talk, especially when children are competing for talk time with one or more adults or older children, their turn-taking abilities may be inadequate. Sue Ervin-Tripp found that in such situations children younger than four and a half years both interrupted and were interrupted more often when adults and older children were present and also talking than when they were talking to one other child, and that they were less successful in repairing interruptions than were older children.[15] The young child has difficulty in following the fast-paced exchanges of two or more other people and thus may intrude with messages that infringe on others' turns or that are seen as irrelevant to the ongoing talk.

At the same time that he is gaining experience with the requirements of transmitting and receiving talk, the child is acquiring the abilities to link what he has to say with what his partner has just said and to tie together his own messages so they are comprehensible to others.

Two girls, who have met for the first time in the playroom, inspect some of the toys. One girl (44 months) begins to arrange some dishes and pans when the other girl (46 months), holding a puppet, approaches her and speaks for the puppet:

Girl (46 months)	Girl (44 months)
Hello. Hello. How are you? (*in a squeaky, puppet voice*).	
	I'm not playing puppet games now.
Why?↘	I don't feel like it.
Why don't you feel like it?	
	Because/ . . . because I don't.
Well, I do. It doesn't make you tired.	
	Yes, it does. It makes me tired, . . . playing . . . um . . . puppet games.
How about play with this? (*Picks up a stuffed animal and shows it to the partner.*)	
	No. I'm not playing with anything except these (*indicates some bracelets found among the pots and pans*). I want these. (*Pause.*) Yuck. I hate these things. (*Throws bracelets down.*)
They're bracelets. They're pretty for you.	
(*Continues to watch partner.*)	(*Turns to another toy.*)

3 / Tracking and Guidance

Talk has evolved as a highly efficient and versatile means of conveying information and attitudes from one mind to another. The tracking and guidance system operates to assure this efficiency and versatility in two ways. First, it establishes reference, that is, it enables a speaker to call forth a concept in the addressee's awareness that is as similar as possible to the concept the speaker has in mind. Reference and deictic terms link talk to events and entities, and through focus the speaker highlights certain elements within a message for special attention. Second, the system must assure that a shared concept is maintained in the course of talk as its status changes from a new referent to a given one and as it is modified. Various cohesive, or tying, devices link the different points in the linear progression of talk.

An example will illustrate the vital work of the system and introduce some of the necessary terms. Imagine two people out walking. One wants to convey to the other that a certain house burned down. The core proposition of his message is composed of a topic (*house*) and a comment on that topic (*burned down*). Since the house, the referent object, is not now visible, the speaker can't just point to it or say "There." He must first establish the house he has in mind as a new topic in his friend's awareness. Just how he does this will depend on his friend's prior knowledge of the house. For starters, then, he must begin by eliciting known information, as in "Remember that old house up on the ridge?" *or* by implanting new information, such as "There used to be an old house up on the ridge." If the referent is assumed to be known and needs only to be brought to the foreground, the speaker uses a definite demonstrative (in this case *that*), but if the referent is being introduced for the first time, it is ushered in with the indefinite article, *an.* If his friend nods or otherwise indicates current awareness of the house as topic, the speaker can then go on to join to it the comment, saying, "It burned down last winter." He maintains the now shared topic by use of the cohesive device of anaphoric reference, that is, a word that refers back to an earlier message component; the proword *it* can now economically represent "that old house up on the ridge." The speaker hasn't bothered to introduce the ridge, but treats it as perceptually given, assuming that he and his friend are facing the ridge. The friend could now respond quite parsimoniously, saying, perhaps, "That's a pity." *That* now represents for both parties the proposition, "That old house up on the ridge burned down last winter." The tracking and guidance system has operated to maintain a delicate balance between precision in identifying a referent and economy in incorporating it into the flow of talk. In general, a speaker attempts to communicate just what is needed in the situation and for his objective, no more and no less. To approximate this ideal a speaker must formulate the message to take into account what he believes is in the consciousness of the addressee at that moment and also what he believes is in the addressee's store of knowledge. What has just been said also becomes part of the information currently available to both speakers.

How children learn to use this system is of considerable interest to developmentalists, first because its correct use implies knowledge of the changing states of other people's awareness; second, because the components are very complex; and finally, because a single form, such as *that*, can serve a number of functions and represent distinctly different meanings, as in the example above. And yet children do attempt to establish reference, to introduce a topic before commenting on it, while they are still producing *telegraphic speech*, that is, before they have learned the various grammatical words and forms that play such an important role in referring and maintaining reference. Indeed, even in the one-word stage of development, children may be building topic plus comment constructions either alone or by collaborating with an adult, producing what Ron Scollon has called "vertical constructions."[1] An example of a vertical construction, which also illustrates what appears to be a topic-comment construction, is the following. A child carrying a toy car approached a preoccupied adult.

Child	Adult
Car (*showing car*).	
	(*No response.*)
Car.	
	(*No response.*)
Car.	
	Car.
Broken.	

The child patiently repeated the name of the referent object, attempting, presumably, to direct the adult's attention to it. (With her second and third repetitions, she was also attempting to repair the breakdown in normal turn-taking caused by the adult's failure to respond.) When at last the adult indicated that he understood what she had said, she added the critical new information as comment on the now established topic. The technique was less elegant than that used by the adult in the example of the house on the ridge, but was functionally equivalent to it. The child did successfully perform a rudimentary act of referring in the process of producing the vertical construction.[2] What leads to this accomplishment, and how does the ability to refer precisely and efficiently develop?

REFERENCE

Words refer to concepts of events, objects, or relationships. A referring expression is one that identifies the concept, distinguishing it, ideally, from any competing alternatives. Just how and when children become aware of reference in this quite demanding sense is not precisely known, but it is certainly several years after they have shown the ability to name events, objects, or relationships and, thereby, to align another person's attention with their own. The ability to indicate an entity for attention, for either one's own or another's benefit, is the first step, and it appears early in the second year of life. Most children at that age point at objects, look at an adult, point again, and look back, as if to check that the adult is attending to their indication. Many children have an idiosyncratic indicating vocalization that accompanies the gaze and pointing and sometimes comes to replace the gestures. These vocalizations are distinctly different from the sounds the child uses to request an object; in fact, they are more often associated with giving or showing an object than taking it. They are usually replaced in a few months with more conventional indicating words such as "look" or "there" or "that." This procedure for calling attention to an object has been called quasi-reference. With it, the child is now ready to throw himself enthusiastically into the naming game, which most caregivers are more than willing to play.

The naming game usually centers about some object of shared attention—a picture book, picture cards, or toy objects—and the objective is to provide a label for each entity. Child–caregiver pairs often develop a routine procedure. Anat Ninio and Jerome Bruner have provided a detailed description of such a routine in the interactions of one mother and her child over the age period from 8 to 18 months.[3] The caregiver points to a picture, saying, "Look." When the child looks, the caregiver asks, "What's that?" If the child responds at all, perhaps with a point, a smile, an unintelligible vocalization, or the correct label, the caregiver provides the label, "It's a dog" or "Yes, it's a dog," and often follows that move with further feedback, "That's right." If the child's response is clearly wrong, the caregiver may correct it and/or provide the correct label. As in other types of verbal interactions, the caregiver becomes more exacting as the child learns to respond; at first, any response will be accepted, then any vocalization, then only the correct label. When the child initiates the first round of the game by pointing at a picture and perhaps vocalizing, the caregiver interprets the child's gesture as a request for a label and promptly furnishes it. Again, as in other child–caregiver games and routines, the child, once he learns the sequence of moves, often exchanges roles and begins to lead the game himself, although in this routine the child never provides evaluative feedback of the caregiver's label.

As practice in learning the rudiments of referring, as opposed to simply learning the names of objects, the game has the advantage of demonstrating, over and again, the appropriate conditions for referring. The first move, "Look," draws attention to a referent object; it presupposes that the attention is not already shared. The second move, "What's that?" presupposes that attention is now shared and directed to what is indicated by pointing and by saying "that." Furthermore, in the labeling move, if the caregiver provides it, or in the feedback move, if the child provides the label, the caregiver is likely to furnish an example of the appropriate anaphoric proword, for the entity: "It's a dog" or "They are dogs." The game grows with the child, and in somewhat more mature forms the caregiver goes on to add or elicit from the child a statement about the referent: *A:* "Yes, it's a dog. What is he doing?" *C:* "Running." *A:* "He's running" or "The dog is running." Thus the repetitive framework of the familiar procedure provides models of continued reference, which contain cohesive devices and predication.

The child has still other cues to assist him in understanding how words are used to refer and to continue a reference. A caregiver is quite consistent, at least in the context of joint play with objects, in highlighting the referent object for the child. She is likely to talk about the object the child is manipulating or which she is showing to the child. She is likely to group the messages about the referent object in temporally discrete and temporally integrated chunks. Observing children between the ages of one and two with their mothers, David Messer found that the mothers' speech about a focal object formed little episodes, with short pauses between messages about the same object and longer pauses when a new object was introduced.[4] And in the course of the episode, the forms of reference changed as the object passed from being a new entry in the field of their attention to being an old or given one: *A:* "Oh, that's a super car. You like cars, don't you? What are you going to do with it? Are you going to make it go?"

Looking at, pointing at, or even holding an object, however, may not indicate the precise referent. How does the neophyte player of the naming game learn that the intended referent is the dog, say, and not the dog's tail or even its wag? In almost all cases (about 90 percent of the time) the caregiver's first label for any picture or object that the pair is attending to is a name for the *whole* object or person rather than a name for a part of it, as Anat Ninio discovered in a study of book reading by Israeli mothers and children of different ethnic origins.[5] Ninio also observed a common phenomenon in caregivers' speech to children: the choice of the label is at the level of abstraction likely to be most useful to the child. The caregiver says, "It's a dog," *not* "It's a poodle" or "It's an animal." Thus the child usually hears the term he is most likely to need in referring to those entities in his daily life.

The child does receive a good bit of help in learning the difficult notion of using words to refer. The available evidence suggests that by the age of two, a child understands that having the addressee's attention is a prerequisite to successfully indicating an entity, and he probably realizes that the means of referring to a particular entity can change over the course of talk. Between the ages of two and three he is becoming aware, though not consciously, that meanings, or concepts, are the substance of talk and are in some ways detachable from particular words and actions. (This latter type of awareness he exercises in his renamings and transformations in pretend play.) He is still, however, not fully in command of the idea that a new entity in the field of joint attention must be identified, not just named or otherwise indicated, and he is not yet ready to identify a new entity in a way that distinguishes it from competing alternatives, if they exist in the situation. It is not surprising that having just mastered the naming game, he is still under the impression that he is naming, an activity that captures the class membership of the entity, rather than identifying, one that selects a certain member of a class. He must now learn the consistent and contrastive use of the indefinite and definite articles, respectively, to identify a new referent for an addressee and thereafter to treat the referent as known.

Several experimental studies have investigated when children exhibit the ability to mark information as new to an addressee (even when it is familiar to the speaker) and subsequently as old, or given. In the most recent study Hazel Emslie and Rosemary Stevenson found that four-year-olds used *a* to introduce a new referent and *the* for subsequent mention of it just as consistently as did their parents, but that even three-year-olds distinguished identifying and definite expressions correctly. The investigators used a simple task, asking the subjects to tell a story about events pictured sequentially on three cards to a listener who could not see the cards.[6] Comparison of their results with those of a prior study, in which the age of acquisition of this skill was set at five years or older, suggests that even for older children, the nature of the task and of the materials can still present obstacles to correct referring.[7] Emslie and Stevenson's results also show that children are learning some of the rather subtle qualifications to the basic rule of *a* for first mention and *the* subsequently. For example, unique entities can be introduced into the field of attention as definite and specific, as in "the moon" or "the air," and some entities entail the existence of others, which latter can then be introduced as definite and specific, as in first mention of "the wheels" or "the engine" after one has just said, "I bought a new car." These types of definite reference involve conventional understanding of what everybody presumably knows—that there is only one moon we could be referring to and that cars are normally furnished with wheels and an engine.

As children begin to introduce topics of their own choosing into conversations, they encounter problems in selecting a referring term that identifies the concept they wish to establish. We might expect fewer problems to arise as long as the talk focuses on the here and now of the physical environment when both child and partner still attend primarily to present objects and actions in progress. But even in this period children and their caregivers must establish precisely what the child intends to refer to. The frequent episodes of "topic negotiation" in which the caregiver offers possible interpretations of what the child has in mind, attest to this fact. During the third year of life, however, children develop an interest in using terms that are descriptively or factually precise. In the following example it is not the selection of the referent object per se that is at issue because both children can see the object; it is a question of what exactly the object should be called. Tom (32 months) and Judy (31 months) were making shapes out of playdough. Tom held up his shape and announced:

Tom	Judy
Look what I made, a "D."	
	That's a moon. It's a moon.
A half a moon.	
	A half a moon.

Judy did not accept Tom's initial name, "a D," for the semicircular shape he showed her, so she proposed another term. Tom accepted it in part but modified "a moon" to "a half a moon"; this was the *mot juste* and Judy accepted it. The referent object was identified with an image familiar to both children.

This is an example of one type of "displaced reference," or what Elinor Ochs Keenan and Bambi Schieffelin have called "nonsituated reference" in their study of the problems children face in establishing different kinds of discourse topics. Children begin to talk about referents that are not actually present in the situation but that exist in fantasy or imagination, or they talk about actual referents that they remember. The former type, Keenan and Schieffelin suggest, appears more often in child–child talk and the latter type more often in child–adult talk.[8] Events from the past can be reexperienced together in talk if and only if the speaker can find the terms to retrieve the event from the partner's memory. In the following example, Jack (32 months) tried to find a term that would help his mother recall something he had seen; the referent was retrieved only through a prolonged cooperative effort. Jack, in the kitchen with his mother, noticed some yellow flowers painted on a pot and commented that they were like his friend Anne's flowers. There followed twenty exchanges, of which I present only an abbreviated version here:

Jack	Mother
(*Points to a flower on the pot.*)	
This is like Anne's flower.	
Like at her house.	
	Where does she have flowers like that at her house?

They're in the drawer. In a
drawer. I like . . . underwear . . . drawers.

You like *what?* ↗

Underwear drawers.

Oh, you mean these flow-
ers are like on her underwear.

Those are on her under-
wear.

Right. On her "big girl"
pants.

On her big girl pants.

Now I know what you're
talking about.

And another one,
Mommy. (*Points to another
flower on the pot.*)

When Jack finally retrieved the image he had in mind, the
topic was now shared, and the two went on to discuss the
color of the flowers on the present pot and on the absent
underwear.

The location of the referent object or event (in the
physical environment, in memory, or in fantasy) is only
one factor in successful referring. Another is the field of
potentially competing referents. In some everyday situations it is necessary to use a referring expression that un-
ambiguously selects a referent from among others that
differ from it on one or more dimensions or attributes. To
select John (the referent) from among a group of boys on
the playground (the nonreferents) so that the other person could identify John, it would be necessary to distinguish John's size, posture, or clothing from those of the
other boys. Then one could refer to John as the tallest
one, the one who is sitting down (if the others are all

standing), or as the one wearing the hat (if all the others are hatless). Any description of John, no matter how faithful, which did not point out a unique attribute that differentiated him from the others would be inadequate. And, of course, it would be ineffectual to direct the other's attention to some attribute that was not perceptually available, such as saying that John was the one with all the cavities or the one with a sense of humor. Furthermore, as the speaker rarely comes up with the "ideal" description on the first try, he must be able to adjust his message to take account of feedback from the addressee that reveals that the description was inadequate or indicates how it was inadequate. The addressee might say, "But I see *two* boys with striped shirts." If the original speaker understands the addressee's problem, he might go on to say that John is the one with the blue-and-tan striped shirt, thus eliminating the boy with the red stripes as the last competing alternative.

Studies of referential communication using tasks that embody some or all of the features of the situation sketched above have revealed that children's performance as either speaker or listener continues to improve throughout the elementary school period.[9] Nursery school children generally perform poorly on such experimental tasks, probably because they do not understand the objective; in this very special and demanding use of language the burden of communication is shifted to talk alone. In most everyday interchanges, ambiguities are either undetected or are resolved with adult help or by the use of richer contextual cues, and the motives for communication are related to the child's own immediate goals. But in this type of experimental task, the message must be self-contained and more precise. The child must be able to mentally compare various items and their attributes without becoming distracted from the task objective. Thus the problem is by no means a purely linguistic or even a communicative one. Perhaps most important, the speaker must take into account the information available to the listener and be able to relate the listener's feedback on the task and modify his message to take account of the need for specific information. Executing and integrating these skills and exercising a critical attitude toward the message itself are formidable tasks, even for the child in elementary school. At any age, however, performance on such a task usually improves to some extent when the listener provides feedback that highlights specific inadequacies of the message.[10]

DEIXIS

The use of indicating terms, such as *here* and *this*, is a convenient verbal shorthand for pointing out components of a situation without actually naming them. Every language has deictic terms. As Kenneth Kaye has suggested, "The power to refer without having to agree on the lexical meaning of terms may be the reason for the universality of deixis."[11]

The ability to refer without using a specific lexical item is certainly advantageous to the young language learner, who can elicit the names of things by pointing and asking "That?↗" And it is useful to caregivers, too, in their daily interchanges with the child. In fact, in assisting the child in a simple task such as putting together a puzzle, the caregiver's use of a full referring expression may confuse or distract the child, whereas a pointing gesture and the instruction, "Put it there" or "It goes there," may be much more useful. The appropriate use of deictic terms requires only that the addressee pay attention to some situational component that the speaker can indicate by verbal pointing, as in "What's this?"

The classes of situational components that can be indicated by deictic terms are the roles of persons: *I* for speaker and *you* for addressee; locations: *here/there, near/far, in front of/in back of* (or *behind*); entities: *this/that;* and time: *now/then, before/after.* The verbs of motion, *come/go* and *bring/take* are deictic in that they indicate direction of motion within the situation. While there are some apparent exceptions, such as "May we come in?" said by a person outside to someone inside a house, the direction of motion is toward the speaker in *come* and *bring* and away from the speaker in *go* and *take.* All the deictic terms, as a matter of fact, are ego-centered; that is, they are more or less anchored to the primary reference point, the speaker. But it is the *role* of speaker to which they are anchored, not to any particular individual.

Although each of these classes of deictic terms is conceptually somewhat different and poses particular problems for the learner, the classes share the following characteristics: 1) they are dependent on the situation for interpretation; 2) they refer to the speaker's perspective; 3) terms within a class exhibit polarity, or contrast, as in *near* versus *far;* and 4) most are not only contrastive but relative as well. For example, *near* may be within the speaker's reach or within a ten-minute drive from his house, depending on the topic of the discourse. The meanings of the terms can be interpreted referentially only by the participants in the speech situation or from their perspective. By way of illustration, imagine finding a note on the street that read, "I will meet you here tomorrow at the same time." The finder cannot interpret this, although it was completely intelligible to the original passer of the note and to the recipient, who would know exactly who *I* and *you* are, where *here* is, what day *tomorrow* would be, and what would be the *same* time, since this information was contained in the situation to which the note referred. Deictic terms thus point outward, signaling to information located outside the text of talk, rather than to elements established within the text. Young children, who are more accustomed to interpreting talk through the situational context than to locating needed information in prior talk, should have little trouble using deictic terms. But the fact that the referent object of a deictic term shifts with a change of speaker causes some initial difficulty, because the young child's perceptions, it is believed, are either anchored to self or do not clearly distinguish between self and others. Even with the assistance of gestures (and only the deictics *this/that* and *here/there* are sometimes accompanied by pointing), it may be hard to grasp where *here* is and who *I* is. *Here* and *I* probably seem to the young child to follow mother about when she is speaking. *Here* is not the same place when mother is sitting next to one and when she is seated across the room from oneself.

A prerequisite to understanding person deixis is self-awareness, the concept of self as a separate entity. This understanding begins to emerge at about 18 months of age, and one of its earliest verbal realizations is the use of *my* and *mine* to assert possession of objects. It may be that the first step in apprehending shifting reference is for the child to get a firm hold on the concept of speaker, and then, starting from the position of self, learn when *I* or *my* indicates self (when self is speaker) and when they do not (when the speaker is someone else). This appears to be how the understanding of *I/you* comes about. The child as speaker uses *I* and *my* correctly, and he understands that *you* means himself when he is addressed by others. In some homes the caregiver attempts (though usually inconsistently) to bypass this first tricky shift by addressing the child by his proper name and referring to herself as "Mommy," as in "Mommy's busy now. Johnny will have to wait." Some children do use their proper names in place of *I* or *my*, and most do address the caregiver as "Mommy" rather than as "you." But even for these children, *I* comes to replace the proper name when their utterances begin to be longer than two words. Proper names are then limited to their functions as vocatives or as designations of third persons (neither speaker nor addressee). They may first use *I* in set phrases, such as "I want————," but they soon use the deictic term for speaker independently and correctly. (I count as a correct indication of speaker role the use, favored by a few children, of *me* in the role of agent, as in "Me sit down.")

In a study of twenty-one girls (ages ranging from 18 to 30 months), each recorded at several visits over a two-month period, Rosalind Charney recorded both spontaneous talk and behavior in a series of comprehension tasks. She wanted to determine the order of acquisition of first-, second-, and third-person pronouns and to learn when the children grasped the idea of the person roles—speaker, addressee, and other human participant. Charney found that when the child was the speaker, she used first person correctly more often than second person, and used second person correctly more often than third person. In respect to comprehension, each girl served as addressee and as nonaddressed listener. She was asked in one task to point to the correct picture out of three (of the child, the mother, and the experimenter) under which an object had been placed. The experimenter would say,

"It's under my picture," or "It's under her picture," or "It's under your picture." The children best understood the second person (*your*) when the child was the addressee. In fact, in this situation they made no errors. They also understood the experimenter's use of the first person (*my*). All of the children made more errors in understanding *her*, whether it referred to the mother or to themselves (when they were the nonaddressed listener). Errors also occurred on *my* and *your* when the child was not being directly addressed.

Comprehension of the first- and second-person pronouns, then, depended on the child's role. As speaker, *I* was acquired first; as addressee *your* was best understood. The children in this study initially learned the pronouns that referred to *themselves* in both speaker and addressee roles. The concept of the reversal of pronouns with change of speaker developed soon thereafter. As Charney put it, the child "learns his position vis-à-vis others before he learns that the roles can be reversed."[12]

After the child understands the reversible positions of speaker and addressee, he can acquire the other deictic classes. The locative terms *here/there* are learned first, followed by *this/that*. These classes are used often in everyday interactions with caregivers in which things and events in the perceptual environment are the primary topics of talk. Use of temporal deictic terms develops somewhat later, although children appear to understand *now* before the contrastive term *then*. Similarly, *close* (or *near*) is understood before *far*. Although no single principle explains why one term within a set would be more learnable or easier to understand than another, there is some tendency for the term most closely associated with the speaker's position and own immediacy to be acquired first; thus *this*, *here*, *near*, and *now* are probably more perceptually salient than their more distant counterparts. But the child must understand both members of each set and their dimension of contrast before the system is completely mastered.

Full comprehension of the contrastive meanings of the deictic terms may be a rather late development. Depending on the type of task presented, children as old as seven or eight may have difficulty with the verbs of motion, *come* versus *go* and *bring* versus *take*, with the use of *in front of/in back of,* and with the use of *this/that* to refer to elements established within the text of talk. Just what a speaker means by *in front of,* for example, is subject to some confusion, as the point of reference may be the speaker or some other object, and that object may or may not have an obvious "front." Cars do have fronts (as do typewriters and people and animals), but if you are facing a car, standing several yards away from it, facing the driver's door, and you ask someone to stand "in front of" the car so that you can take a picture, it is not the rules of language but the rules of common sense (and cooperativeness) that lead the person to stand between you and the car, rather than at the front end of the car.

Young children's use of deictic terms may, for several reasons, give the impression that they comprehend the terms better than they actually do. First, they never make mistakes concerning the various classes. Children understand and use *this/that* to refer to entities and *here/there* to refer to locations. In fact, they learn the locative meaning of *here* and *there* before they use the terms to indicate the nearer-farther contrast in location. The actual spatial scope of either term is relative to the topic, and if no contrast is intended, both terms are quite flexible, so the child's failure to grasp their polarity may not lead to misunderstanding.

Second, children often hear and use redundant indicating phrases, such as, "Go away" and "Go for a walk." While sitting on the floor with her mother, Sarah (25 months) decided she wanted to have a story. As she got up to fetch a book, she turned back to her mother and said, "I'll go and get a book. Stay there, Mom." "Go and get" was probably an unanalyzed phrase for Sarah at this time, and, so, perhaps, was "Stay there." It might have been a phrase her mother used when preparing to leave a room; very probably Sarah did not select the deictic term to indicate her mother's location while she herself moved away.

Third, other types of redundancy may not only lead to the impression that children actually are using *this/that* contrastively but may also assist them in understanding the polarity. For Sarah, *that* was associated with *over there*, so that in emphatically re-asking her mother to identify an object equidistant from both of them, she pointed and said, "That. Over there." Mothers of still younger children have been observed to favor *that* and *there* as they point to or handle objects with the child, presumably orienting toward the child's proximity to the object. When *this* and *that* are used as demonstratives, the contrastive meaning is present, and these forms are likely to be stressed. Both Sarah's mother and her friend Becky frequently modeled this contrast for Sarah, as when Becky, directing Sarah, said, "I talk on *this* phone. You talk on *that* phone."

Fourth, children do have some grasp of the general pragmatic principles concerning the types of statements or questions usually directed to different persons. This knowledge was displayed in the typical errors children made in a study conducted by Christine Tanz.[13] When she asked children to relay a question to a third party, they had to shift the pronoun appropriately:

Experimenter asked	Child should ask	Typical error
1. Ask Tom where my bike is.	Where is her bike?	Where is your bike?
2. Ask Tom where you should put this.	Where should I put this?	Where could you put this?
3. Ask Tom if he is tired.	Are you tired?	

The type-3 question produced virtually no errors. Although fewer than one-third of the children made any errors, the more common errors may have been influenced by what the children knew of the normal use of language. First, a type-2 question about the child *himself* ("Ask Tom if you've been good") was often not relayed, especially among the younger children. Instead, they answered it, "I've been good." After all, the self should know this information better than the unfamiliar third party! Other type-2 questions using *should* or *could*, as in the example above, were sometimes not transformed; in these cases Tanz speculates that the children understood *you* to mean *one* or *anyone*. Errors on type-1 questions resulted in asking Tom a question, not about the experimenter (*her*) but about Tom himself (*you*); perhaps this error reflected the children's knowledge that one usually asks people about information that they, and they alone, should have ("How old are you?") rather than what they might know about another person ("How old is she?").

COHESION AND COHESIVE DEVICES

At about their second birthday, children begin to link their talk both to what a partner has just said (reactive linking) and to what they themselves have just said (proactive linking). Little episodes of coherent talk, which have been called "islands of coherence" in the stream of verbal and nonverbal behavior, begin to appear, and with them appear the signposts and landmarks that are cohesive devices. A minimal interactive episode is defined as a sequence of two reactively linked exchanges. Among the first of such episodes that Sarah (26 months) engineered while playing with her friend was the following (the subscript $_r$ is used to keep track of nominal reference):

Sarah	Becky
Where's your baby?$_r$	
	Right there. (*Points to doll.*) That's$_r$ my baby.$_r$
What you gonna do to her?$_r$	
	(*Occupied with fixing the baby bottle, Becky doesn't answer.*)
(*Turns to the toy telephone and murmurs into the phone.*)	

Sarah began by presupposing the existence of the referent (*baby*) and asked about its location. Her failure to first introduce the referent caused no problem since Becky had recently put the doll in its cradle. Becky replied with a deictic expression, a physical gesture, and then a deictic and a noun phrase. Both girls correctly shifted speaker and addressee pronouns in this exchange. Becky's response was coherent in that it did indeed address and reply to the question, and it employed the cohesive device of lexical repetition in the repetition of *baby*. Sarah's second question was also coherent in that she asked a *next* relevant question to continue the episode. In doing so, she maintained reference by using the pronoun *her*. This cohesive device signals co-referentiality with its antecedent, *baby*; that is, *her* and *baby* both refer to the same referent object.

Pro-forms, ellipsis, and focus. One type of cohesive device serves to track referents through subsequent mentions in a text and generally to reduce redundancy as well. To this type belong anaphoric reference, substitution, and ellipsis. All of these direct the addressee back to a point in the text where the more fully specified form can be found, or at least back to the point where the referent entered the discourse via a deictic term. The personal pronouns, demonstratives, and comparatives (*same, such, other, else, more*) are used for anaphoric reference. Devices for substitution, in which an expression is replaced by a substitute of the same grammatical class, include nominal (*one, ones*), verbal (*do, do so, do it*) and clausal substitutes (*so, not*). For simplicity I will combine anaphoric reference and substitution, calling them proforms. Ellipsis is simply the omission of some part of what was said before. The addressee can find the missing material by tracking back in the text to the more fully specified form. These devices operate on given material and are usually unstressed; in the case of ellipsis some or all of the given material simply vanishes, leaving only a signal (usually a fragment of a clause) that points back to what is presupposed. These devices operate very intimately with the component of focus, which indicates the prominence of an element in a message. New information is focused usually by means of louder stress and/or by pitch placement, although syntactic devices may also be used to focus an element. Old information is less prominent. Focus may also operate across messages; loudness and/or pitch may mark an element in one message as standing in contrast to a similar element in a prior message.

Before the age of two, many children understand that two or more events occurring in succession may be related, perhaps because they share some, but not all, features; these children will reduce the prominence of the shared (or old) information while indicating the new information through focus. The child uses intonation as a cohesive device before he acquires the pro-forms and the system of grammatical ellipsis. Halliday provides an example of contrastive focus as used by his son Nigel, who wanted his mother to put his cereal on his own little table. Primary prominence in each utterance is indicated here by italics.[15]

Nigel	Mother
Put Bemax down on *table*.	
	It *is* on the table (*the adult's table*).
Nila table.	

In his first message Nigel used normal intonation, in which the last stressable syllable of an utterance is given prominence. His mother replied using a pro-form and using contrastive prominence on the verb *is*, by which she contradicted Nigel's implication that the cereal wasn't on the table. Nigel replied by emphasizing the new information, contrasting Nigel's table with the other table. Having realized the relation of coherence, and having one means of marking it, the child will over the next year or so begin to use at least some of the pro-forms and some elliptical patterns in continuing reference to old information.

But should Nigel be credited with ellipsis (as well as cohesion via focus) in his reply, "*Nila* table"? Presumably his mother and any listener could expand his message to mean "Put the Bemax down on *Nigel's* table."

Probably he should not be so credited, since it is unlikely that he himself could expand his message to its full form (although he certainly did mean to convey that full message). Furthermore, the rules for ellipsis would dictate that he include the preposition *on* in his reply, "On *Nila* table." Very young children often respond to adult questions with minimal messages, as in, *A:* "Are you hungry?" *C:* "Nope"; or *A:* "Where's the baby doll?" *C:* "Right here." It is doubtful, however, that these types of responses alone represent control of grammatical ellipsis, for children at this period also produce incomplete messages that do not conform to the linguistically defined rules of ellipsis, omitting, for example, finite verbs: *A:* "Are you a good baby?" *C:* "I good."

Between the ages of two and a half and three and a half, however, children begin to systematically delete textually presupposed information and to use pro-forms, and the "equivalence" of elided and full forms can often be observed in the children's speech. Thomas Thieman asked a group of children between the ages of 44 and 66 months to repeat and then to recall a number of sentences, some of which were presented in full form and some in grammatically reduced form. Although all the children could repeat the full forms correctly, when they were asked to recall the complete sentences, in 55 percent of their responses they transformed the full forms to more compact forms. Even when asked to repeat, in 31 percent of their responses they transformed full forms to reduced forms. The youngest child of the group, however, spontaneously transformed the reduced forms to full forms and failed to reduce those sentences presented in full form. For example, on hearing the sentence, "The bird sat in the tree and it sang a song," the child produced a fully reconstructed version, "The bird sat in the tree and the bird sang a song." An older child remembered the sentence as, "The bird sat in the tree and sang a song." She went one step beyond the model, omitting the pronoun *it*.[15] While deletion and reduction by means of pro-forms within a sentence follow many of the same rules as ellipsis and use of pro-forms in discourse, it is necessary to examine coherent episodes of talk directly to determine when and how children actually use these cohesive devices. To date, very few studies have attempted to answer these questions and to determine whether full and redundant messages are preferred before elided or reduced messages become more common, as they are in adults' coherent texts.

The three- to five-year-olds we studied used almost all the possible types of ellipsis in their talk, the commonest being omission of the entire clause, retaining only the polarity marker (*yes* or *no*) as the signal. Twenty-two percent of all their utterances used ellipsis. The following table shows the types of ellipsis, beginning with those most frequently employed in the speech of all the children and ending with the rarest. An example of each type is presented along with the percentage that each type represents of all those children's elided utterances.

Type of signal retained	Example	Mean percentage of all elided utterances
1. Polarity marker	Are you ready? Yes (I am ready).	40
2. Modal element	Can you see it? I can (see it).	13
3. Wh component	There's only one thing to do.	11

Type of signal retained	Example	Mean percentage of all elided utterances
	What? (is the one thing to do).	
4. Logical connective	Why don't you want to do anything? (I don't want to do anything) 'Cause I'd rather be back at school.	9
5. Complement	What do we have to use? (We have to use) A raincoat.	7
6. Subject	What's in there? Cookies (are in there).	6
7. Matrix clause	Where did the table go? I'll show you (where the table went).	6
8. Adjunct of clause	Where's the man? (Is the man) At the factory?	2
9. Lexical verb	I go get some ice cream after my mommy comes. You won't go (get some ice cream after your mommy comes).	2
10. Simple verb	There's no play houses. Yes, there is (play houses).	2

The three-year-olds and the five-year-olds used about the same proportion of elided utterances; the major difference between the groups was in the proportions of the types. Whereas 50 percent of the youngest children's ellipses were signaled by a polarity marker, which is a very simple, prefabricated response requiring no special construction, only 30 percent of the older children's elided utterances were of this type. They were beginning to use the other types more frequently. Still, as the table indicates, the preferred types (1–4) utilized a signal that was one of a finite set. Once the set was learned, its members could be used in an indefinite number of elided responses. The polarity markers include *yes* and *no;* the modal elements include *can, will, do, did, is (am, are, was, were)* and their negative forms, *can't, won't, wasn't;* the *wh* component includes the question words *who, where, what, why;* and the logical connective signals include conjunctions such as *but, because, or.* Between the ages of three and five the use of the *wh* component and the logical connectives increased significantly (and the use of the polarity marker decreased significantly). While the children in both age groups were using ellipsis to about the same extent, the older children were becoming more versatile in the types they employed. Another interesting finding was that two-thirds of the children's elided utterances were reactive; in most cases the presupposed material occurred in the prior speech of the partner. By the age of three, then, children are using this cohesive device in constructing interactive text.

There are two reasons to reject the idea that ellipsis *results* from the inability to remember prior messages. First, ellipsis is highly patterned and not a random phenomenon, as forgetting parts of a prior message would be, and second, in most ellipses it is the end of the message unit that is elided, the part that would be most recent in short-term memory. One might ask, however, whether the information that has been deleted from the surface structure of the message is actually forgotten. Do children who are exchanging elided messages, "Yes, you are"—"No, I'm not," for the third or fourth time remember the sense of the full form, such as, "You're a scaredy-cat"? Could they restore the deleted portions, as would be the case for adults? In some cases the answer is yes, they probably could. We found in our study of ellipsis that in 18 percent of the elided utterances previously omitted material reappeared either fully or partially in subsequent speech within the same episode. This phenomenon, combined with lexical cohesion, is illustrated in chapter 1. The following example of two five-year-old boys shows both full and partial reappearance in both proactive and reactive relations. (Elided material is in parentheses.)

Boy	Boy
I'm not going to do anything.	
	Why? (aren't you going to do anything).
(I'm not going to do anything) 'Cause I don't want to (do anything).	
	Why don't you want to do anything?

Material can be restored after a few or after several elided utterances. The younger children produced a somewhat higher percentage of reappearances than the older, although age differences between the groups were not significant.[16]

In further studies of the cohesive devices that reduce redundancy and maintain reference in coherent talk, we found that anaphoric reference using pronouns was most frequent (56 percent of all reductions) and that using demonstratives (*this* or *that*) the next most frequent (21 percent). Substitution (*one, do*) and comparatives (*same, other*) were used quite rarely. Since the children did reduce redundancy on second and subsequent mentions of nominal referents, we wanted to discover the conditions under which they failed to reduce it. We suspected that the presence of the referent object or entity in the immediate speech situation would facilitate the "normal decay" of the full form of a nominal reference to a pro-form, but that other factors might inhibit the tendency to reduce a noun phrase during continued reference. Nominal referents were introduced into the conversational episodes as definite (*the car* as opposed to the indefinite *a car*) in 74 percent of the cases. Referents were less frequently introduced as indefinite, the form that might be expected for new information probably because children tend to talk about objects that are perceptually present to both partners. But whether introduced as definite or indefinite, most referents were reduced in subsequent mentions. The presence of the referent object in the situation made reduction more likely, but even when the referent was absent, reduction took place, although the older children reduced more consistently than the younger ones. Interestingly, if the referent object or entity was make-believe, reduction tended to be inhibited, especially in the younger group. Other conditions that blocked reduction to a significant extent were adding a new referent to the episode and adding new information to the referent, usually in the form of an adjective. Reduction was highly unlikely when the speaker failed to obtain an acknowledging response from the partner and when the pair failed to agree on the identification of the referent.[17] Children between the ages of three and five are beginning to use this type of cohesive device (particularly pronominalization for anaphoric reference) in a discriminating fashion, varying the form of reference to reduce redundancy when possible, but maintaining a more complete expression when there might be confusion or miscomprehension.

Conjunctions and particles. A second group of cohesive devices provides information about how a response relates to a prior message. These devices do not reduce redundancy but may be used in combination with the pro-forms and ellipsis. This group includes the conjunctions, which indicate the logical or semantic relations between successive clauses; the discourse particles, which indicate semantic and pragmatic relations between messages; and some intonation patterns, such as successive tone groups with rising intonation, used when one counts or lists items in a series. The conjunctions used frequently in coherent episodes of interactive talk by almost all children during the preschool years are *and, because, so, then, but.* There is considerable variation in the patterns of acquisition, that is, whether these connectives are used first to link messages between speakers or within one speaker's turn or his own complex sentence; the different meanings expressed by these connectives; and the age at which they are first used.

The first connective to appear in children's talk is *and,* which occurs first in proactive and a little later in reactive linking, at about two years of age. It is also the first connective to link phrases and clauses in the single speaker's construction of complex sentences.[18] *And* is most frequently used to link messages in a simple, additive relation, and it is often associated with sequences of actions or collections of entities. This use is probably supported by the common adult question: "And what else?" (do you see/have/want). As a first, all-purpose connective, and for many children the only explicit connective for several months, it may on occasion reflect other meanings as well. It may imply a relation of temporal succession or simultaneity, as when Sarah (27 months) brought her mother a book and said, "Would you read it to me? And I'll listen," or it may imply a relation of causality, as in, "Hold the ladder and it won't fall down."

Four major classes of relations between events have

been distinguished, and it is these that the child must grasp in order to use the connectives. They are the relations of addition, of temporal dependency, of causal dependency, and of contrast or antithesis. Before the child begins to use explicit connectives, he may simply juxtapose messages, and in many cases his understanding of the relation can be inferred in the context. Later the child will express the relation by using a connective. In the case of causal relations, it has been found that when the child gives some evidence of understanding a causal link (at about two years of age), parents begin to ask *why* questions. Next the child begins to answer them with messages introduced by *because*. Around the age of three, children ask *why* questions themselves and begin to formulate complex messages dealing with cause and effect. Some children reflect a preference for effect-cause ordering of messages both before and after they learn to use explicit causal connectives. Sometimes, of course, simply saying *because* or *just because* with no further elaboration serves as a child's answer to a *why* question, and often the quality of the logic may be a bit suspect, as in the following example (which also illustrates ellipsis) from the pretend play of two boys, each three and a half years old.

Boy	*Boy*
I'll take care of the fire, okay?	
	Well, I will 'cause I'm the fireman.
Well, I'm the fireman 'cause I want to be the fireman.	
	Okay, then you can have that. (*Hands partner a block.*)

As this example shows, *then* is also used to express causal dependency, and *so* is added to the repertoire. The first meaning of *so* can best be paraphrased as *in that case*, and some children use *then* with that same meaning, as Sarah (28 months) did. (Note also Sarah's problem with the pro-forms in her second message.)

Sarah	Becky
Whose purse is that?	
(*Points to a dress-up purse.*)	
	This purse is yours.
Then is that your purse	
yours? (*Points to a second*	
purse.)	
	This purse is mine, yes.

A rather later development is the use of *so* to express the meaning *so that* and, even later, *therefore*, as when a three-and-a-half-year-old, busy cooking a monster in the toy oven, commented to her partner: "I don't see any ground beef on him, so I have to put him back in the oven."

But first expresses contrast, or the adversative relation. Its first meaning is that the following message is an objection or consideration incompatible with the prior message. A girl examining a stuffed animal commented to a boy, "He looks like a mouse." The boy replied, "But he has stripes," and she agreed, "Yes, he does," admitting to the implication that mice don't have stripes. (The animal was in fact a tiger, with whiskers.) Like *because* and unlike *and*, *then*, and *so*, *but* is first used to link the child's message to another person's speech (reactive use) before it is used to construct complex, single-speaker messages. Like all the other connectives, *but* expresses several different nuances. Ann Eisenberg, who has followed the development of connective use and meaning in the speech of several children between the ages of two and four, points out the increasing use of the "Yes, but———" response when a child acknowledges another's position but continues to maintain his own opposing view or desire.[19]

Discourse particles, the little words that relate a speaker's response to a prior message and add subtly to the meaning of the response, begin to appear in two-year-olds' talk. Both *well* and *just* can contribute to cohesion, and both prove very difficult to define in the abstract; their precise meaning on any occasion is intimately dependent on both the text and the context. This is also true for several adverbial particles that may, but need not always, presuppose a prior message and thus function cohesively. These include *again, still, already, yet* (more often, *not yet*), *though, too,* and *just* in the sense of *just now*. In Ann Eisenberg's longitudinal observations, the average age of first use for *well* was 34 months, and for *just,* 30 months. For the adverbs, *again* appeared first at the average age of 29 months, and the others at about three years.[20]

The friends Judy, Jack, Tom, and Anne also used these particles at an early age (although Sarah had not yet begun to use *well* or *just*). I will briefly discuss only the uses of *well* and *just* in their talk. *Just* appears at first in two related meanings. One sense, which can be classed as *only*, diminishes the importance or offensiveness of an event. It is used in mitigating a request, in replying to an accusation, or excusing a refusal. When Anne asked Jack (32 months) to give back her necklace, he kept it, saying, "I'm just breathing on it." The other sense indicates emphasis and is often used to call attention to what follows as particularly relevant to another's prior behavior. Anne (34 months), for example, spoke sternly to her naughty doll, "Will you just go to sleep?" and she told Jack for the third time not to push her, saying, "Just stop it." The phrases *just a minute* and *just like* were also used and were probably unanalyzed lexical units.

Well occurred first in one of the meanings common in the mothers' talk with these children; it indicated that the upcoming reply might be unsatisfactory to the addressee. Judy (33 months) refused an invitation by Anne, "Let's go to a airport," by saying, "Well, I'm gonna stay here with my baby." The second early use was to express impatience at a partner's delay. For example, Jack's mother had asked Jack (30 months) if he wanted an ice cube from the refrigerator. He said he did, and she replied, "Okay," but didn't immediately get up from the floor where they were sitting. Jack said, "Well, get up!" Both of these uses are accompanied by slightly rising intonation.

Lexical selection. The third type of cohesive device is lexical selection. It does not necessarily reduce redundancy, but it may provide texture through repetition of words, use of synonyms or paraphrases, or selection of words associated in one semantic domain. The principles of association may be hierarchical, as when the dog, Randolph, is subsequently mentioned as "that animal," a superordinate term, or as "this fine otter hound," a subordinate term to the more general *dog.* Such flexibility in hierarchical relations is not common in children's talk, although on occasion a superordinate term seems to trigger a number of subordinate members, particularly in the framework of pretend play. A girl (37 months), in the role of Mother to her partner's Baby, decided to go get "groceries" and immediately began to ask Baby whether they needed milk, whether they had butter, and whether she should get bread, waiting after each question for Baby to nod yes or no. (The names of roles or role relationships portrayed in pretend play are capitalized to distinguish them from actual persons, except in direct quotations of children's speech.) Children are likely to use certain general nouns that indicate classes of nominal referents, such as *stuff* or *things* for groups of objects, and *people* or *kids* to refer to several individuals who have been mentioned separately in previous messages.

The term *place* provides a cohesive link to expressions indicating location, as in the following exchange. Jack (32 months) asked Anne (34 months) if he could sit on a little chair at the snack table, and she replied, "No, that's baby's place," as she placed the doll in the chair.

Two types of lexical cohesion are common in the talk of young children. One is akin to the collection of grocery items mentioned above; lexical items that have a close semantic association for the children are clustered in the same episode, although no clearly superordinate term is expressed. A common collocation for the three-year-old group reflected the semantic domain of illness or, more generally, "not being well." For example, the same child who as Mother was going grocery shopping was playing with some small cars when her boy partner (39 months) brought the teddy bear over to her and announced:

Boy	Girl
I got my poor teddy bear.	
	(*Stands up to look at the bear.*) Is he sick?
No.	
	Well, what's the matter with him then?

Boy	Girl
He's not . . . he's too tired to . . . (*Climbs on car with bear.*)	
	Put him in that big bed. (*Points to the sofa.*)

The attributive *poor* appears to have called up the chain *sick, the matter, tired,* and *bed;* the pattern of associations was shared by both children. Other pairs used these semantically related words, as well as *don't feel good/well, temperature, a cold, doctor,* or *medicine* (see the first example in Chapter 6).

One pair of children began a long discussion when one girl said, "I'm sick," and the other replied, "I'm sick, too." This exchange illustrates the use of repetition, the second type of lexical cohesion common in children's talk. At the same time this exchange typifies the process of matching, whereby children create coherent interchanges. Matching often employs repetition, but its basic principle of organization is more general. The rule for matching might read, "To respond to a partner's message, assert of yourself what your partner has asserted of himself, with whatever modifications may be appropriate." Lexically cohesive items are usually repeated, but there can be considerable flexibility in moving from one matching exchange to a next one that extends the pattern. The following excerpt from a longer episode, which contains a number of different cohesive devices, produced in a playful mood by Judy (thirty-two months) and Tom (thirty-three months), illustrates the matching technique. This interchange stretched the children's linguistic capabilities almost to the breaking point and involved considerable self-correction, which has been edited out here, indicating the difficulty of formulating such an episode of "pure" talk. It began when Tom announced, apropos of nothing,

Tom	*Judy*
I'm very bigger.	
	I'm very little.
My mouth is bigger than yours.	
	Well, I'm not bigger yet 'cause I'm walking down the street yet.
I'm not very big to walk down the street yet, either.	
	Well, not like me (*giggles*).
Uh, my mouth is little, too.	
	Well, my mouth is bigger.
I got a little smaller shoe.	
	I've got big sneakers just like Mickey does.

(The episode continued with exchanges in which the children contrasted their sizes with those of Mickey or Dicky; Judy does have a pair of Mickey Mouse sandals.)

The various cohesive devices help organize text, or coherent discourse. Children begin first to tie talk to its immediate context, to objects and actions, but very soon thereafter they also begin to link talk to their own and others' just prior speech. The prerequisite to this achievement is, of course, the ability to sustain attention to an object or event singled out by the self or by the partner. The linguistic means for indicating continuity of reference, pro-forms and ellipsis, require a number of years to master, and the connectives and subtle particles that indicate just how messages relate to one another and to the context or the speaker's attitude reflect quite complex concepts. Nonetheless, at least some of the members of each class of device appear during the latter part of the third year of life, and the frequency and diversity of these devices increase rapidly over the preschool period. The use of these devices does not wait on the acquisition of mature syntax, as the preceding example illustrates. It appears to grow along with the use of talk and the development of the other linguistic components of language.

Having a real tea party in the playroom, Judy (32 months) and Tom (33 months) very politely share the orange juice and chocolate-covered peanuts.

Tom	Judy
Would you like a choco-late-covered nut, too? (*Takes one from the bag he is holding and hands it to her.*)	
	Yes, please. (*Begins to eat it.*) Ummm . . . ummm (*eating noise*).
Here's a nut. Want it? (*Hands her another.*)	(*Takes it.*) Ummmmm. (*Hands him a little plate.*)
Thank you (*Sigh.*)	
	(*Hums.*)
(*Hums, giggles.*)	
	Have the bag? ↗
(*Doesn't hand over the bag, but gives her another nut.*)	
	That/ you have to save for later.
Another one? (*Hands her another nut.*) I hold the bag.	

The children take turns humming and making ummmm ummmm noises, and then these change to an exchange of mock growls.

4 / The Facilitation System

Talk could not operate without a facilitation system to reduce friction and minimize the potential conflicts and embarrassments that can arise in social contact. This system reflects the speakers' ritual concerns and their pervasive awareness of interpersonal status in the transactions of daily life. The operation of this system is as ubiquitous as the societal organization it mirrors and supports. It includes the use of little markers of courtesy and concern such as *please, thank you,* and *excuse me;* displays of attentiveness and understanding during a talk engagement; selection of acceptable forms of address and phrasing of requests; and selection of topics suitable for the occasion. The speaker's manner of speaking and acting conforms not only with his achieved and ascribed status, but also with his role relationship with the others in the situation. Talk adjusts to the stable social relations between speakers and also to the more transitory ones, as when two strangers must discuss a common task or plight, or when a child adopts an authoritative tone when explaining to his mother how to play a pretend game he has devised.

Such obviously polite expressions as *please* or *excuse me* are only the tip of the ritual iceberg. Their appropriate placement in a strip of talk is a matter of considerable delicacy. Although most parents coach young children and even prod them to produce these phrases under the conditions that call for them, the phrases are unlikely to be used reflexively in all the appropriate contexts until the child has learned their ritual functions. In the case of *excuse me* and its equivalents, *pardon me* or *sorry*, the child probably has been told that he should say "excuse me" when he has bumped into someone, when he walks in front of someone, and even when he wants to interrupt an adult's speech. Thus he could learn that *excuse me* is required for small offenses; that it should follow an accidental offense; and that if he must commit an intentional offense in order to do something necessary, *excuse me* should precede the offensive action. He will probably also sense that correctly placing *excuse me* before an offense is associated in some way with certain special ways of requesting and of asking for permission, such as saying, "May I————" or "Can I————," or "Let me————." He may even have grasped the notion that these rules are more frequently enforced if the offended person is an adult than if he is another child. But learning the proper placement of the apology requires a more generalized knowledge of what constitutes an offense in the first place and of how the relative status of the persons involved influences the gravity of an offense. This knowledge, which every normal, socialized person possesses, whether he chooses to violate the basic rules or not, the child will only slowly acquire from observation, trial and error, and from some limited rule formulation by adults that will only partially explain the principles underlying any instantiation of the tacit code of conduct.

There are at least two large areas of social convention and organization that are relevant to talk and that are often reflected in language form, that is, in the various linguistic alternatives speakers may select. One area is the differentiation and ranking of persons and the types of role relationships that are recognized. The other area is that of the commonality, the generally accepted properties and rights, of persons, or at least of all persons who are recognized as members of the group for whom the conventions are valid. The two areas are intricately interrelated, and they may be organized in different ways in different cultures and social groups. In this chapter I will discuss some of the implications for talk of person differentiation and of person "appreciation" or proper consideration. First I will describe the two areas and the points at which differentiation and appreciation operate in tandem. Next I will discuss requesting, which is a social act that sensitively reflects both fine distinctions in relationships and awareness of proper conduct with others. Finally, I will discuss how one type of request is associated with the relationships between persons and their relative status.

HOW PERSONS ARE DIFFERENT AND HOW THEY ARE THE SAME

The differentiation and relative status of persons has been described as varying on two dimensions, that of relative power and authority in which persons are superordinate, subordinate, or the same in rank, and that of relative distance, in which they are close (familiar, intimate) or more distant (unfamiliar, lacking shared interests or attributes). Stereotypically, at least, it might be expected that parent and child would be ordered as superordinate to subordinate and would be familiar or intimate. A husband and wife might be equal in rank in one cultural group and superordinate–subordinate in another, but they would behave as intimates in both groups. A judge and a lawyer in the courtroom might exhibit behavior appropriate to a superordinate-subordinate relationship that was distant and formal, but the same two persons as friendly competitors on the tennis court would interact in a relationship of equality and familiarity. A number of languages, including German, French, and Russian, provide contrasting sets of pronouns that reflect both of these dimensions, thus incorporating the distinctions into the structure of the linguistic code.[1] Some languages, such as Javanese, provide alternative lexical forms of verbs and nouns as well as an elaborate pronoun system. Some languages, such as English, do not provide alternatives in the pronoun system but mark the distinctions by terms of address, for example, Judge Strong, Your Honor, William, Bill, and Billy. All languages provide some means by which speakers can differentiate among persons and relationships.

Languages also provide means for members of the cultural group to recognize and acknowledge the membership, or "personhood," of others and to differentiate among degrees of agency and responsibility. Fully responsible members of the culture take for granted a shared knowledge of the conventions of thought and action, and even shortcomings in someone's behavior can be excused or reinterpreted on mutually intelligible grounds.[2] Less-than-full-fledged members are dealt with, and spoken to, in a different manner. The apt phrase "speech to incompetents" was proposed by the linguist Charles Ferguson to designate the several speech styles, or registers, that exist in most cultures for talking to or with persons who are not fully accredited members.[3] "Speech to incompetents" includes the registers used to communicate with babies and young children, with the senile and the infirm, with the very ill, with pets, with prisoners, and with foreigners who have not acquired the language or cultural conventions of the members' group. Each of these registers differs from the others in a number of important ways, but they share certain characteristics that stem from members' expectations that these classes of individuals are not fully capable of engaging in "normal" communication and other common social transactions.

Members of a culture accord themselves and others, except for these less-than-full-fledged members, the full ritual consideration due to capable and responsible persons. Such persons can be trusted (except under conventionally extenuating circumstances), to observe the guidelines of the cooperative principle in action and in talk, can be expected to fulfill the given-new contract, to have a fine awareness of others' opinion of them and a desire to maintain or achieve a favorable opinion, and they will know what rightfully belongs to themselves and will accord similar rights and authority to others. They will cooperate with others in maintaining their own and others' personhood, in part by appropriately recognizing differences in relative status. Talk, along with other forms of public action, will display and confirm (or may disconfirm) this image of the self. In order to say, "Excuse me" at the right time, at the right place, and to the right person, a speaker must know what constitutes an offense against the self and thus against another person who is a comparable self. A part of this normally taken-for-granted knowledge has been explicitly stated by Erving Goffman in an essay entitled "The Territories of the Self."[4] Intrusion on or infringement of any of these territories can count as an offense and thus require an apology and/or an accounting of some sort.

THE TERRITORIES OF THE SELF

The concept of claims, of what belongs to a person, is central to social organization and to understanding social behavior. The territories of the self described by Goffman form a preserve to which a person can lay claim; that is, he is entitled to possess, control, use, or dispose of it. One's territories include not only spatial configurations, inalienable and alienable possessions, and belongings protected by institutional or legal sanctions, but also temporary, private, and psychological "possessions." The territories include one's personal space, a sort of invisible ellipse about oneself that varies with the situation and activity; the "stall," or place being used, such as a seat at table or in the theater, to which one can lay claim even if temporarily absent; use space, or "elbow room," the area needed for specific purposes such as positioning a car for parking, mopping a floor, or building a sand castle.

Less evidently physical or spatial territories include one's turn, that is, the right to be served or to talk in some order relative to others; the "sheath" of skin and clothes; possessional territory, or personal effects, which includes matters relating to one's comfort, such as sound levels, lighting, and temperature; the information preserve, which includes what one is thinking, one's private history, "good name," and correspondence. Finally, there is the conversational preserve. Part of this preserve is the right to control, to some extent, who can summon one to talk and when. To this list I will add an extremely variable, but very sensitive, preserve of the time and effort a person can expect to call his own, somewhat comparable to use space. Intruding on someone else's time requires apology or permission, such as, "Have you got a minute?" Some claims radiate out to other persons who "belong" to the self, such as wife, family, gang.

The extent of all these territories varies with the situational context, of course, and with a person's rank relative to others. Compared with adults, children enjoy less extensive rights not only in respect to space, but also in respect to information and conversation. Almost any adult can ask a child, "What's your name?" "How old are you?" or "Is Johnny Mills your brother?" An adult, however, must go to considerable trouble to assure that he does not offend an unfamiliar adult of presumably equal status if he wants to ask a similar question: "Excuse me. You look terribly familiar. Could I ask if you happen to be related to John Mills?" Showing several marks of person appreciation, the adult apologizes for intruding into the other person's conversational and informational preserves, provides an account in advance of his need to risk this offense, and then asks permission to intrude with a question that also actually conveys the request for information.

In learning about the territories of the self, an area of social knowledge that requires many years of experience to control, the child will gradually discover what constitutes an offense, what requires apology or an accounting, and when he must try to mitigate or excuse an offense before committing it. Other ritual matters are also tied to the concept of territories of the self. One function of saying "Thank you," for example, is to recognize another person's offering or giving of something that the person could rightfully claim or reserve for himself, such as giving up a seat or place in line. Person appreciation, which has been summarized in the rules "Be polite, don't impose, and give options"[5] rests, to a large extent, on knowledge of the territories of the self. But how and when does the child acquire this knowledge that every adult possesses, but which few could "explain" in so many words? Most caregivers believe that it is very important that the child learn to "ask nicely" and "be polite," but they could no more provide the child with the underlying rationale for saying "excuse me" than could the child understand such an explanation. What caregivers do is prompt the child in specific circumstances to say the proper ritual phrases, as in "Say 'Thank you.' "[6] They also make some judgments of specific offensive behavior, such as, "It's not nice to stare at people," and provide cautions about invading another's territories— "Don't bother Daddy. He's studying." And many caregivers and teachers model appropriate phrases and polite forms of requests in speaking to children, "Wouldn't you like to put the toys away now?" perhaps in hopes that children will reciprocate the courtesy. Children do learn a great deal about appropriate forms of requesting during the preschool years, as will be discussed below. There is very little direct information, however, on how children learn about the territories of the self.

It is known that children acquire the concept of possession of objects very early; *mine* and *my* are among the first linguistic formulations of the concept, and the concept can often be inferred when the child indicates an object and provides the name of the possessor, "Daddy hat." In resolving conflicts over physical possession of an object, nursery school children appear to be influenced by whether the taker has had prior possession of the object, the "prior possessor" being less vigorously resisted.[7] In respect to the concept of use space, Grace Wales Shugar and Barbara Bokus have shown that three-year-olds have a keen awareness of the boundaries of their own and their playmates' activity spaces, the areas in which they are playing and to which they have some rightful claim. A child playing with one partner was able to show an investigator by marking on the floor or placing little objects, the heretofore invisible circle of his own and his partner's play space. If the two children were playing together, the child would delineate a single, elliptical space that enclosed both, usually with most of the space between them. When the children were not engaged with one another, the child would draw a circle about himself (with a radius of about an arm's length), with himself in the center and would draw a separate, slightly smaller space for the other child. When asked where a third child could play in the room, the child would indicate another area, separated from the space assigned to self and partner together or to self and to partner independently.[8] The children also indicated the spaces differently in talk. They used deictic expressions to refer to the activity space of a separate partner or to a shared activity space, "That's her place" or "This is ours," but they favored descriptions in referring to their own separate space, "I'm working here. My store takes all this room." In another study of spontaneous play sessions, these investigators found that pairs of children used two different types of utterances in initiating interaction. If the children were farther apart, a child was likely to initiate talk by an ostensive type of utterance, "Look. See this." If the children were closer together (less than 65 centimeters), the initiation was likely to be descriptive of the speaker's activity, "Tracks and wagons for a train, I'm making." These findings of both verbal differentiation and gestural indication of the relation of self and others' activity spaces and the awareness that activity was either common or independent suggest that these aspects of the territories of the self are salient for preschool-age children.

It is consonant with the general trends in development of social cognition that children begin to understand about the territories that are either perceptually given or delimited by their own actions before cognizing those territories that are less overtly marked or less related to physical action, such as the information preserve. The notion of the turn, although highly variable by situation, is one that even young children appear to recognize if the rights pertaining to the turn apply to themselves. Their concept of turn, however, is at first probably restricted to turns at acting, as in sitting on the swing or using a toy, and that is the type of situation in which caregivers urge children to take turns.

REQUESTS FOR PERMISSION

The following example illustrates how a caregiver models socially acceptable speech and attempts to guide a child's behavior. (The example also shows that the caregiver's precepts, even when followed, do not necessarily result in an experience that might reinforce the child's attempts to be polite.) Tom used a type of request that solicits permission and thereby acknowledges an addressee's authority and/or his claim to a preserve. A conflict arose between Judy (32 months) and Tom (33 months), who were alone in the playroom. Tom wanted to have a little figure of a bear that Judy was holding, which Judy refused to give him. When Tom began to cry for his mother, Judy's mother came into the room. Tom whined a couple of times and then explained his distress to Judy's mother, who directed Tom to ask nicely and reminded him of the turn-taking rule. She also used a polite version of a request to Judy in urging her to comply with Tom's request.

Mother	Tom	Judy
	(*To mother*) I want that little bear.	

OK, well ask Judy nicely for him. You can take turns, I know.

(*To Judy*) Could I have that little bear?

No, no, wait till I'm finished.

(*To Judy*) But I want the little bear.

(*To Judy*) Judy, if you're not playing with the little bear, why don't you give it to Tom?

(*Judy mumbles but does not relinquish the bear.*)

(*Facing mother and Judy*) I want it.

(*Looks at bear and around at other toys.*) Oh, there's the bear, here's something . . .

(*Still facing both mother and Judy*) Can I have it? (*Points to bear Judy has just dropped.*) I wanna see the bear.

(*Mother puts another toy near Tom and leaves the room.*)

Mother	Tom	Judy
	(*Temporarily dis-*	(*Stands, watching*
	tracted, he examines	*Tom.*)
	a toy camera.)	

(*As soon as the mother leaves the room, Tom turns toward Judy and the bear, and Judy moves once again to defend her claim.*)

Tom, don't you touch my things, all right?

When Judy's mother told Tom to "ask Judy nicely" for the bear, he complied by requesting Judy's permission to have it. All requests share the essential feature that the speaker wants the addressee to do something; requests for action involve some act that the speaker desires or some behavior that will bring about a desired state of affairs. Requests for information are designed to lead the addressee to provide information in a verbal reply or a gestural equivalent. In requests for permission the addressee is asked either to allow the speaker to do or have something or to cease obstructing or preventing the speaker from doing something. Tom certainly could have complied with Judy's mother's request by issuing other polite requests, "Will you give me the bear?" or "Please give me the bear." I suspect that his choice of a request for permission in, first, a more polite variant ("Could I have that little bear?") and, second, a somewhat less polite one ("Can I have it?") was influenced by his recognition of Judy's prior claim to the bear and/or her mother's ultimate authority in deciding who might play with what.

If young children do choose to use requests for permission for particular social reasons, then we might expect the requests to be used when the addressee was in some way obstructing the speaker from doing or having something he wanted, or when the addressee had some rightful claim to what the speaker was interested in. This proves to be the case. Among the forty-eight pairs of three- to five-year-old children we observed in the laboratory playroom, there were 121 instances of forms conventionally used for requesting permission, "Let me————," "Can I————," "May I————." Of these, 108 instances were complete, uninterrupted, and clearly addressed to the partner (rather than to a doll or an imaginary interlocutor); 87 percent of the complete instances occurred in situations in which the addressee was either physically obstructing the speaker in something he wanted to have or do, such as sitting on the car the speaker wished to drive, or appeared to have some claim to what the speaker wanted. The claim was established either by just-prior use or by the statement of a plan to use some object; for example, the addressee had just finished an imaginary phone call and turned away from the toy phone when the speaker asked, "Can I call on it now?" Some claims seemed to be related to the conventional association between the sex of the child and the particular toy; for example, a boy pointed to an ironing board that the girl had not previously touched or used and asked, "Can I have that?"

If a speaker uses a request-for-permission form, he is actually requesting the addressee's permission, but if the addressee is physically obstructing him, the speaker is also less explicitly requesting the addressee to cease the obstructive action. If the addressee must take some other action in order for the speaker to achieve his desired objective, the addressee, if cooperative, will also perform that action. Thus if the addressee was sitting on the wooden car in the playroom and the speaker standing near it asked, "Can I ride on the car?" or "May I ride on it now?" and the addressee grants permission by saying "Yes" or "Okay," he would also either get off the car or move to the front or back, thus allowing the speaker to get on. The permission request leaves it to the addressee to determine what action is required. Almost all of the three- to five-year-olds observed in the laboratory playroom enacted this ritual interchange when one wanted to sit on the wooden car, which was the most popular toy in the room. No child simply granted permission by saying "Okay" or "Yes, you can" and then failing to move. Although the addressee complied in 70 percent of these interchanges, noncompliance often reflected the addressee's understanding that he had some prior claim to possess or dispose of the desired resource, "You can in a minute," "I'm not through yet," or, "It still my turn."

Although in the last example Tom requested Judy's permission at the initial urging of the adult, all the two-and-a-half-year-olds negotiated similar interchanges without adult prompting. In the following example, Tom (33 months) and Judy (32 months) negotiated Tom's activity in the pretend cooking that Judy had initiated. Tom approached Judy on the floor where she had set out plates and cups:

Tom	Judy
Can I play here?	
	Yeah, you can.
(Sits down by Judy and points to a plate.) Can I have some muffins?	
	Don't touch them, 'cause they're very hot.
I'm gonna put a little sugar in your muffins, all right?	
	(Judy watches as Tom pretends to sprinkle sugar on the imaginary muffins.)

Tom appears to have recognized and verbally acknowledged Judy's right to her own play space and her right to control the pretend activity in which she was engaged. Once he was allowed to join, he was still cautious, and she reminded him that she was still in charge. Not all of the two-and-a-half-year-olds' interchanges were so ritually correct, but the talk of all of these children did on occasion reveal that they could, unprompted by an adult, take into account another's claim to activity space, objects, and turns at acting. The right to ride on the wooden car, an issue in many permission requests, provided sequences of requests and rerequests that displayed the children's ability to paraphrase this well-motivated directive. Among the formulations used to gain access to the car were the following: "Can I have a turn now?" "Let me get on there? ↗" "Hafta have a turn, please," followed by "I really should be driving this," "Can I do that, please, now?" and "When it stops I can do it? ↗"

REQUESTS FOR ACTION

In any directive act a speaker risks infringing on another's preserve, and for adults there is potential danger of offending the other person by a presumption or of causing embarrassment to the other or to the self in the event of a refusal. Languages offer a proliferation of alternative forms for issuing directives, forms that allow the speaker to accommodate to the social situation. I will list the major options and some of the variants that are available to adult speakers of English, discuss the conventions and understandings associated with the use of directives, and then trace the development of requesting in children's talk. Although directive speech acts include requests for information, commonly formulated as questions, and requests for confirmation, agreement, sympathy, and evaluation, it is the request for action (RA), or behavioral request, that is perhaps the most ritually sensitive type. It is certainly the type that has been the most widely studied in both children's and adults' speech, and I will restrict the following discussion to requests for action.

The basic direct linguistic form for an RA is the imperative, either positive, "Eat that," or negative, "Don't eat that." Other forms can be ranked on the dimension direct/explicit, indirect/inexplicit; in general, the greater the degree of indirectness, the more "polite" the request. The appropriateness of a particular request form depends on the relationship of the speaker and the addressee, the context of the request, and the tone of voice employed; however, it is not possible to predict that a given request form will be taken as polite or offensive without knowing the situation. The major options available to adults for requesting an action are listed below in roughly descending order of direct to indirect; possible variants that may seem more polite are listed last in each group.[9]

Imperative: Give me a glass of milk. You give me a glass of milk. Give me a glass of milk, please.

Need statement: I want a glass of milk. I need a glass of milk. I would like/I want you to give me a glass of milk.

Imbedded imperative: Will you give me a glass of milk? Can you give me a glass of milk? Would you give me a glass of milk? Could you give me a glass of milk?

Permission directive: Can I have a glass of milk? May I have/Could I have/Might I have a glass of milk?

Question directive: Is there any milk? Have you got some milk? I don't suppose you have any milk, do you?

Hint: That glass of milk sure looks good.

This listing is partial, of course; the reader can add other possibilities, such as, "You better give me a glass of milk," "Don't forget to give me a glass of milk," "Why don't you give me a glass of milk?" "Could I ask you for a glass of milk?" Also, in the home, nursery school, classroom, or wherever the standard operating procedures are familiar to all participants, reference to a rule or procedure can convey a request for action, as in, "You didn't give me a glass of milk," or "I don't see a glass of milk at my place," or simply, "Milk time," while holding out an empty glass.

Young children who have not yet mastered the more standard forms listed above have a few verbal means for conveying requests that cannot be ranked as either direct or indirect, since in the child's repertoire they do not yet contrast with other standard forms. The most common of these are: a statement with rising terminal pitch, "You read it↗"; the simple imperative form of the verb, "Read," or "You read"; or the name of a desired object, "Milk," perhaps with an appropriate gesture. Two other rather early forms that continue in use for several years are *you hafta* or *you gotta* plus verb, as in, "You hafta read book," and an interrogative tag appended to a need statement or an imperative, "I want it, okay?" or "You sit here, all right?↗"

By the age of seven or eight, children are able to place the standard options and their variants in appropriate contexts and assign them to appropriate persons in different role relationships, as Claudia Mitchell-Kernan and Keith Kernan found when they asked black American children between the ages of seven and twelve to make up stories and enact them, using puppets as the characters in the role play.[10] Nurses interacted with patients; fathers with wives, sons, or daughters; and customers with salespersons; the children also interacted with each other outside the puppet play and with the investigators as well. The directive forms they used varied with the relative status of the persons, with the personal versus the transactional nature of the engagement, and with the cost in time or effort that compliance with the request demanded, for example, "Hand me that wrench" (low cost) versus "Belinda, will you go to the store for me?" (higher cost) when speaker and addressee were same-age peers. The investigators also observed that the children sometimes used inappropriate directive forms, apparently to test, negotiate, or redefine a status relationship. When a child directed an imperative RA to the investigator (normatively inappropriate recipient) and received a non-compliant response (and perhaps an objection to the rudeness), the child would rerequest in a more polite form. These observations indicate that the children understood a good deal about the social implications of directive choice. And although the relative status of the participants is an important factor in selecting the appropriate option or variant, more transitory features of the interaction, such as the cost of the requested act to the addressee and whether the act would be normally expected or counts as a favor, also influence the selection. Favors are usually requested more politely than are acts the speaker considers obligatory. Probably skill at effective use of RA options continues to be elaborated through adolescence and beyond.

What do children know or learn about the practical, everyday business of directing others and of being directed that allows them to acquire such a complex set of options and variants? No single answer is available at this time, but some features of requesting make the system a bit more learnable than it might seem to be at first glance.

First, I suggested above that children are in the process of learning about the territories of the self and about what might constitute an offense or an imposition on another person. Second, many of the RA options encode some of the social understandings about the practical action of requesting and about understanding a message as a request. These understandings are: 1) that the speaker (S) wants the addressee (A) to do some desired act (DA); 2) that the DA should be done for some purpose; 3) that A has the ability to do the DA; 4) that A is either obliged to do the DA or is willing to do it; and 5) that S has the right to ask or tell A to do the DA and that A is an appropriate recipient of the request. A further understanding is that if no specific time is mentioned, the DA should be done at the time of speaking. Speakers and addressees also understand that requests are only validly made for future acts and for acts that the addressee was not intending to perform anyway.[11]

These understandings are not linguistic in nature, but they are encoded in part, at least, in many of the RA options. The embedded question forms with *will you* and *can you* encode understandings 4 and 3, respectively. Need statements stress the speaker's desire but do not encode the fact that the addressee is expected to perform some act to fulfill the need. Understanding 1 is encoded in the expanded imperative, "I want you to give me a glass of milk." The children's form *you hafta* encodes the understanding of obligation, and the permission directives recognize that the addressee may have a claim that conflicts with compliance. Thus some of the social understandings that underlie requesting are encoded in talk, and they are also made more or less explicit in the talk that precedes and follows a request in the children's everyday interactions. The several meanings present to some degree in

any directive act may be expressed in the RA message itself, as a preparatory message for the request, in the response to the request, or even in a reformulation of an
unsuccessful directive act.

Caregivers use most of the different options in speaking with their children, although they use hints and
question directives less frequently with younger children.
They also encode many of the underlying understandings
in replying to children's requests and in the episodes of
interaction that usually accompany a request. It is not
surprising that very young children most frequently use a
need statement ("I want more") to make requests of
caregivers, since caregivers expand a child's gestural
meaning and simple demand of "Milk" by saying, "Oh,
you want some milk" or "Do you need more milk?" or
"What do you want? Some milk?" Refusals may also encode the understandings: "I can't get it right now" or
"You already have some milk, you don't need any more."
Further, in preparing to make a request or in explaining
the request, the caregiver often provides one of the associated meanings. Jack's mother, for example, stated the
purpose, or need, for the request before using an indirect
RA: "I don't have any lemonade. You wanta pour some
for me?" Many similar experiences are necessary before a
child begins to learn that expressing one of the associated
meanings of a directive act can, under certain circumstances, count as a request. Thus the third type of help
the child might receive in learning about the forms and
meanings of requests derives from the negotiated nature
of directive acts and the clustering of the related forms
and meanings in talk exchanges with caregivers.

It is neither necessary to suppose nor probable that
very young children comprehend the linguistic meanings,
let alone the subtle interpersonal nuances, of the various

options and variants they hear. In fact, Marilyn Shatz has shown that two-year-olds have an "action bias"; they are likely to perform a physical act if they detect an action word in an utterance and if it is possible to carry out the act the word denotes.[12] Thus, concerning comprehension of the different forms of indirect requests, probably the very young child does not understand the complete message in requests by caregivers even when his compliant behavior indicates comprehension. For example, it may matter little whether a mother says, "Can you jump?" or "Would you like to jump for me?" or "Did you see the rabbit jump?" The child is likely to respond by jumping if the situation permits. But between the ages of two and three, the child's increasing sensitivity to a speaker's intention and his growing comprehension of the linguistic meaning of phrases used in directive messages make it possible for him to learn from the often redundant linguistic and situational cues that are grouped together in negotiated directive episodes.

A complicating factor in comprehending indirect directives is that most of the more polite alternatives are indeed ambiguous. One reason they are considered more polite is that the addressee can understand and respond to them in more than one way: he is given an option, in effect. He can respond to the more literal reading and its force or to the intended directive force or to both. For example, a teacher's utterance to a nursery school child, "Would you like to play on the train?" could be understood as an offer meaning, "I'll let you play on the train," or as a polite directive meaning, "I want you to play on the train." In an experiment Kenneth Reeder asked children of two and a half and three years to decide which alternative force was intended under two different contextual conditions. In one case a puppet child and puppet teacher were facing one another, but the teacher was nearer the toy train than the child; in the other case, the child was near to and facing the train, and the teacher was farther from the train. The utterance, "Would you like to play on the train?" was interpreted as a directive in the first condition (in which the teacher would be sending the child over to the toy) and as an offer in the second condition (in which the child was already near to and looking at the train, presumably interested in it). The two-and-a-half-year-olds were reasonably consistent in this discrimination but were better at judging the offer than the directive. The three-year-olds were more consistently accurate on both judgments.[13] In everyday life children probably use not only such spatial cues but also facial expression, tone of voice, and other information about the speaker and the situation to assess the speaker's intention and thus to clarify potentially ambiguous messages. We would expect that without such cues their performance in interpreting indirect forms would be poorer, as has been found in other experiments.

In the case of many indirect requests in everyday interchanges, older preschool children sometimes recognize both possible meanings. The embedded imperative "Can you————" can be understood as a request for information about the addressee's ability *or* as an indirect request for action. The force of the inquiry about ability may not be totally absent even if the addressee responds to the directive force. A five-year-old boy, for example, handed a girl a cloth tape measure that he had unwound and had tried unsuccessfully to roll up again. He asked her, "Can you roll this up?" Taking the tape measure, she replied, "I'll try, but if I can't, it's your problem, all right?" She recognized the directive force of his message and responded to it by acting and speaking appropriately, but she also verbally responded to the question of her ability to do the desired act. Many request options are not analyzed in this fashion, being used and understood as conventional formulas for requesting, both by children and by adults. Nonetheless, their literal meanings are potentially available to be singled out for attention, or even as the focus of a joke or flippant response, "I can, but I won't."

Children's selection of the directive options and the politeness variants also reflect their awareness of the differences among persons, and specifically, of the relative status of individuals. The differentiation of persons is marked in children's talk and in other behavior in many ways other than the choice of directive, of course, and in some instances the differentiation has little to do with the relative ranking of persons as of higher, lower, or equal status to the child. People who have different functions in the child's life may receive different types of communication. Some children, for example, reserve whining for the principal caregivers and never whine when dealing with teachers, other adult relatives, or other children. Familiarity, or lack of it, is also an important factor. A preschooler is more likely to approach and talk to a familiar adult or child than an unfamiliar one. In chapter 7 I will discuss some of the ways children use to indicate their understanding of the attributes and characteristics of different persons and interpersonal relationships. Here I will briefly summarize how children choose the RA forms according to the rank of the addressee in relation to the speaker.

Imperative RA forms are associated with behavior control, and more indirect forms are associated with asking for favors or high benefit/high cost services. The right to control, exercise authority, or dispense favors is one defining feature of higher status, whether the right is attributable to age, size, strength, capability, or access to valued resources. Children aged three or four use the imperative primarily with younger children; they use more indirect RA forms with adults and children older than themselves. In some homes, at least, fathers receive the more polite RA options and such politeness markers as *please*, while mothers receive need statements and bare imperatives. Imperatives were the most frequent type of RA among all the peers observed in our laboratory playroom,[14] a tendency that is constant through early elementary school, where at least four-fifths of all RA directives to peers are imperative. Older peers use more of the indirect RA options, but the proportion of direct to indirect forms remains approximately the same through the third grade.[15]

Strategies for rerequesting. If a request does not at first succeed, what do children do? They can, of course, simply keep repeating the same request, perhaps more and more insistently. This tactic is certainly common enough among younger preschoolers, but its use tends to decrease with age; by third grade repetition of the same request is used less than 10 percent of the time when a first request fails. Preschoolers do, on occasion, vary their strategies, both in the case of a nonresponse and in the case of a noncompliant response, the latter being the more frequent outcome. The requester's perseverance appears to be related to the importance, or benefit to self, that he attributes to the goal of the request.

In the first example in this chapter Tom, prompted by an adult, used a very polite request (*could I*) to Judy. When that failed, he produced a need statement (*I want*), then another indirect request (*can I*), and finally ended with another statement of need (*I want*). Both need statements may have been meant as appeals to the adult rather than rerequests to Judy; we cannot be certain. The pattern of using a polite form, then following it when it is unsuccessful with *I want* has also been observed in the speech of Scottish children with their parents.[16] And it can be found in most transcripts of children's interactions with caregivers. Commonly, in the *I want* rerequest to parents, the substance of the initial request is reduced or diminished in some way.

Children can adapt to noncompliance in at least four ways. Which change they select depends to a large extent on their relationship with the addressee. First, they can revise the content of the request, asking for less or attempting to make the cost of the desired act appear less to the addressee. This tactic is often used to parents. Second, they can try again more politely in hopes that observance of the ritual proprieties will increase their chances of success. Even two- and three-year-olds, when prompted to do so, can increase the politeness of a request by adding *please* or softening the tone of voice, although older children command a greater variety of the conventional politeness variants and of other techniques used for persuasion. Third, they can escalate the request, making it more forceful or assertive, either selecting a more direct RA option or adding a threat or warning about what the consequences of noncompliance might be. This tactic is often used by dominant children to those less powerful. Fourth, they can accommodate to the formulation of the noncompliant response, taking into account what their partners have said. This alternative can be combined with any of the first three. Once a directive intention has been conveyed, it remains in effect throughout subsequent negotiation, and talk can be directed to the conditions relating to the request and any considerations brought up by the response. This was the tactic that Judy (31 months) finally chose when countering Tom's (32 months) failure to grant her permission directive:

Judy	Tom
(Stands beside wooden car.)	(Driving wooden car.)
Can I have a turn now?	
	(No response.)
I have a turn now? ↗	
	I'm doing it right now.
When you finished? ↗	
	I'm not finished yet.
Awright. (Continues to stand by car and look at Tom.)	
	(Drives for seconds.) Now I'm finished. (Climbs off car.)
(Gets on car.)	

Judy had at least three reasons to exert herself to the utmost to shape her rerequest ("When you finished?" ↗) to Tom's response. First, and probably foremost, he was in physical possession of the car. Second, he had not actually refused her first requests. He ignored one and gave a temporizing response to the replay; thus he did not force her by strong opposition to escalate the strength of her request. And third, as a boy he was in some way entitled to have a say about use of the car. (Despite the number of daily trips to nursery school and on errands in cars driven by their mothers, the majority of the children we observed considered the right to drive and to tell how to drive the car as more a male than female perogative.) Given three such coincident considerations, Judy was highly motivated to adapt her requests to her partner's response.

A final comment on the workings of talk. So much is going on at any one time in the several different systems of organization, it is surprising that it works as well as it does. In addition to the requirements of the several systems, however, there is the real motive force, that is, what the speakers are trying to do. Children are learning how to talk in the context of interpersonal exchanges motivated by objectives they may not yet understand. And yet they enter in enthusiastically and come to understand the significance of talk by virtue of talking. Not only must children be very finely attuned, or biologically adapted, to the properties of talk and to the requirements of the underlying systems, but they must also receive a good deal of help from adults, in a form they can utilize at that particular point in their development. A final example will illustrate the patience, persistence, and humor of a mother and the patience, persistence, and willingness of a child (Sarah at 26 months) as they worked through a problem of what was, essentially, a ritual observance.

Sarah, who was at the age when she might say no to her mother's suggestions, sometimes woke up feeling grumpy. She was also at the age when she was willing to say what she was told to say and to repeat under certain conditions what her mother said. On this morning her mother wanted to change her clothes and said politely, "Let's put on a shirt 'cause this one is dirty." Sarah replied, "Stop it. *NO!*" The following interchange ensued:

Mother	*Sarah*
What did I tell you you had to practice? ↗	
	But . . . yes, yes, yes.

Mother	*Sarah*
Yes (*softly, laughing*).	
	What can I practice?
You can practice, "Yes, mommy, yes, mommy, yes, yes, yes" (*rhythmically*).	
	Yes, yes . . . (*fades out*).
Yes, mommy, yes, mommy, yes, yes, yes (*in same rhythm as before*).	
	Yes, mommy, yes, yes (*with similar rhythm*).
All right, now let's try it. Sarah, may I take off that dirty shirt, please?	
	(*No response.*)
What do you say? ↗	
	Thank you.
No, you don't say "Thank you" (*Laughs.*) You say, "Yes, mommy, yes, mommy, yes, yes, yes."	
	Yes, mommy, yes, mommy, yes, yes, yes (*rhythmically*).
Right now. Can you take it off or do you want me to take it off?	
	I take it. (*And she does.*)

Sarah's willingness to be led in talk helped her finally to achieve both the physical and verbal compliance her mother had intended from the outset of the episode. A previously well-learned lesson, that when an adult says, "What do you say?" the expected response is "Thank you," temporarily interfered with the exercise. Sarah was correct, however, in realizing that her mother's general objective was to obtain compliance and that a ritually acceptable response was also required. And she was also beginning to learn, perhaps, under what conditions a very polite parental request is actually an order that can't be refused.

Working out a conflict of interest, two boys who have met for the first time in the playroom argue about the use of a toy truck.

Boy (40 months)	Boy (44 months)
That's mine. (*Approaches partner who has started to play with truck.*)	
	This is not. No. (*Moves truck.*)
It's mine. (*Stands, looking down at partner and truck.*)	
	Well, I'm using it. I'm using it.
Could I take it home?	
	No, it's the school's.
Yes, I *am* take it home.	
	You don't have a house, you live here.
No, I live at home, Lake Charles Avenue.	
	Well, I'm *using* that. I'm using it.
Could I take that home?	
	Yes, okay. (*But doesn't relinquish the truck.*)
Could I take that home? (*Speaks more softly than before.*)	
	Okay, but/ but/ but I'm using it. (*Turns away from partner.*) I'll give it to you when you're gonna go. (*Continues to play with truck.*)
(*Moves away from partner.*)	

5 / On Saying, in Effect, "No"

Refusing, denying, objecting or prohibiting, and disagreeing may not occur very frequently in most talk engagements, but when a negating response does occur, it is highly salient to the participants. Even the solitary speaker occasionally makes negative comments, remarking, perhaps, on a failure or change of plan or the nonoccurrence of some expected event. Because we do think positively and speak positively most of the time, negation is of particular interest as a special case. Furthermore, not only squabbles and quarrels but also the most highly valued accomplishments of logical argumentation depend on verbally expressed opposition. In this chapter I will discuss first the development of linguistic negation and negating responses, from the determined "no" of the toddler who resists an adult or rejects an offer, to the child's pointing out to a friend that something the friend said is false. I will then go on to examine how children create and resolve arguments. The accounts will illustrate the convergence of affective, cognitive, linguistic, and social factors in talk and also demonstrate how children learn to do more and different things with words.

LEARNING TO SAY NO

Before the child can be credited with a first verbal negation, he will have exhibited resistance to a restraint on his actions, most probably by pulling away from an adult or pushing the adult's hand away. Probably he will also have firmly indicated rejection of a verbal offer of food or a toy by shaking his head. The child generally makes such a response to a perceived intervention in his line of action but he may also reject something that he has previously accepted or will immediately thereafter accept quite happily. These oppositions become more common at about the time the toddler begins to concentrate on doing things for himself, when he begins to move off on little trips of exploration, to attempt to feed himself, and to manipulate objects to enhance their interest. This is the very time, of course, that caregivers must begin to intervene in behavior that is potentially dangerous, destructive, or troublesome. Caregivers begin to say, "No" or "Don't," and the child begins to reciprocate.

This adamant assertion of independence, along with the rejection of adult help, control, or even solicitude, has been interpreted by the psychologist Charles Wenar as a critical step in the development of autonomy and the sense of personal efficacy. It occurs as the self is increasingly differentiated from others and as the self and others begin to be known as agents, as individuals who act with specific intentions. From this period, which Wenar calls Resistance, the child moves on during his second year to exhibit Negativism, defined as "intentional noncompliance to adult requests, directives, and prohibitions."[1] In this period verbal expressions come to complement or even replace head shakes or physical gestures, and the child now discovers many more occasions for oppositional behavior. *No* is one of the first words acquired, and many children use it unsparingly.

The mobile and curious toddler, who is a frequent recipient of parental prohibitions, warnings, and refusals, seeks to defend his own autonomy by resistant or oppositional behavior. At the same time he sometimes succumbs to those very constraints: he begins to prohibit himself! He will say "No" as he approaches the hot stove or shake his head as he reaches for his mother's glasses. Actions that have been prohibited by adults can be subject to self-prohibition (although, true to form, the self often disobeys). Even a slightly older child will betray the influence of a prior adult prohibition, as did Sarah (28 months) who said, while putting a piece of Lego in her mouth, "We don't eat it." Recognizing what has been forbidden has been considered as a first step toward the self-controls of conscience or the internalization of conventional rules for behavior, which are essential factors in the processes of socialization.

In prohibiting his own actions, the child is performing two roles: that of the initiator of acts and that of the restrainer of the acts. These two functions were previously distributed between the adult and the child. But saying "No" either to self or to another has still further significance. It distills a common factor from a number of different, emotionally charged experiences without referring to any single experience or palpable thing. Rene Spitz saw this conceptual aspect of "no" as the first conquest of an abstraction and called it "the most spectacular intellectual and semantic achievement of early childhood."[2]

Other, and even more impressive, functions of negation appear in the second year of life. The child learns to use the words *no, not,* and *don't* with meanings other than rejection, refusal, protest, or prohibition and begins to express some negative meanings in words and phrases that do not contain those negative words. Linguists and psycholinguists have traced the development of the semantics of negation.[3] Although there are some differences in interpretation, there is considerable agreement on the order in which negative meanings are acquired. Recent studies by Roy Pea of the comprehension and production of negation, using both experimental and observational techniques, indicate the following course of development.[4]

Resistance and self-prohibition are among the earliest negative meanings expressed verbally, as well as by gestures. Another, quite different negative meaning, which seems to have no gestural equivalent, is intended when the child comments on the disappearance of some thing or person or the sudden termination of some experience, saying, "Gone," "Allgone," "Stop," or "No more." The comment may be made in response to a question such as, "Where is Daddy?" or "Where is your juice?" or as a spontaneous observation, such as, "No doggie." The child first associates this meaning with his own action, as when he puts an object under a pillow so that it is hidden from view or when he finishes a glass of juice. Later the meaning of disappearance or cessation is extended to events not caused by the child. A related meaning is that of unfulfilled expectation. When an attempt at action misfires, part of an object is missing, or an object is not in its usual place, the child may note the discrepancy by saying "no." He also expresses this meaning when he suddenly abandons a course of action he has been engaged in and starts another. Allison Gopnik has pointed out that these negative meanings reflect the child's ability to compare an event or outcome with an expectation or plan. The mismatch between the expectation or aim and the present reality is the actual referent of this negative expression.[5]

Another type of negative meaning, which emerges a little later, usually at about two years, is the negation of a proposition. *Truth-functional negation* expresses the judgment *That is false*; the words *no* and *not* are used in the important functions of denial, correction, or contradiction. According to Roy Pea, "The grasp of this binary distinction [the truth or falsity of a proposition] is a fundamental touchstone of reasoning and language cognition."[6]

Understanding or formulating the possible relations between states of affairs and linguistic propositions is quite complex. Consider the types of statements that could be made about the simple states of affairs depicted on the right-hand side of Figure 1, where there are two

	Relation	Statement	Selected Referent in Array I
1.	True affirmative	This is a circle	◯
2.	False affirmative	This is a circle	◯
3.	False negative	This is not a circle	◯
4.	True negative	This is not a square	▢
5.	True negative	This is not a square	◯ Array II
			▢
			▢
			▢

1. *Truth-functional statements and their relations to arrays of referents.*

arrays, one consisting of three circles and a square and one consisting of one circle and three squares.

In experiments in which adults and other children are asked to verify statements having the various relations (listed at the left in the figure) to the arrays, it has been consistently found that on measures of errors or of time required for verification, relations 1–4 are ranked in ascending order of difficulty. But it has been shown that relation 5 is considerably easier to understand than relation 4. One reason for this is that in language use, true negatives are reserved for cases in which an affirmative proposition has either been asserted or implied and for cases in which a contrary state of affairs is believed to be the normal situation. Thus one would not announce, "I am not guilty," unless one were denying an accusation or responding to a prevailing opinion to the contrary. What have been called the "plausible contexts of denial" are those situations in which an exceptional item is characterized (relation 5 in array II) rather than an unexceptional item in a situation (relation 4 in array I).

In experiments that utilize simple arrays of familiar objects and in which the task simulates dialogue (the type of language use most familiar to the child), children of three and a half to four years are able to determine the truth or falsity of the statement-array relations. Their responses also show that the order of difficulty of these judgments is the same as it is for adults. There is also some evidence that even younger children are sensitive to the contexts of plausible and implausible denial, that is, they find relation 5 easier to understand than relation 4.

In everyday talk exchanges, children begin to learn about the relations of true and false messages to familiar objects and events. When asked, they must express judgments about the identity or attributes of persons or things in the immediate environment. Simple "yes" or "no" responses suffice to answer a question such as "Is that your nose?" asked by an adult who is pointing to the child's nose or mouth. For some children younger than two years, the first step in learning to use truth-functional negation involves first learning to distinguish questions that require *yes/no* answers from other types of questions. For a short period a child may answer all *yes/no* questions with "yes" or with "no," without regard for meaning. The child simply recognizes that the question requires a response, but not a naming response, and that he must take a turn-at-speaking. This stage is quite brief, and answers to *yes/no* questions soon match with the facts of the case. Truth becomes a relevant criterion for response selection.

THE ELABORATION OF TRUTH-FUNCTIONAL NEGATION

Between the ages of about 20 and 30 months children learn many uses and forms of truth-functional negation, including the elaboration of responses to *yes/no* questions. Children begin to expand their negative responses by providing the correct *positive* formulation. When asked, "Is there another pig in the box?" a child of 21 months, who was searching through a toy box, correctly answered, "No," adding, "This . . . box . . . baby," as she found a doll. This answer exhibits a basic pattern of logical disputation, that is, *not X but Y*, and also reflects a general tendency to restore communication to a positive formulation. Other patterns of elaboration include *not X because Z* and *not X but Y because Z*. These patterns are first modeled by adults to the child in a number of variant forms, some of which omit the explicit denial *not X* or even omit explicit connectives. For example, when Sarah (26 months) named a picture in a book "alligator," her mother corrected her, saying, "It's like an alligator. It's a crocodile."

One pattern of elaboration, *not X because Z*, is also used in elaborated responses to requests or offers. Deborah Keller-Cohen has pointed out that a modal adult response to a child's simple refusal is a probe that requests a reason for the refusal.[7] In such instances the pattern is actually distributed between two speakers, the child replying, "No," the adult asking, "Why not?" and the child then supplying the reason, usually introduced by *because*. This distributed version also occurs in two-year-olds' peer exchanges: Judy (30 months) has just finished drinking some pretend tea that Tom (31 months) has given her. She gets on the wooden car.

Judy	Tom
	You want me to fill you some more tea?
No, thanks.	
	Why?
'Cause I don't need any, 'cause I'm parking the car.	

The elaborated patterns of truth-functional negation, as used in child–adult interactions, are also distributed between the two speakers, a child's simple "no" often receiving a probe by the adult for a positive identification: *A:* "Is that a dog?" *C:* "No." *A:* "Well, what is it?" *C:* "A bear? ↗"

Two-year-olds are already beginning to be flexible in the forms of elaborated denial, sometimes explicitly verbalizing the relations between negative and positive messages and sometimes omitting parts of the patterns.

When Sarah (27 months) put her dolls to bed and covered them, her mother suggested she read them a bedtime story. Sarah asked her mother to read the story, but her mother refused, saying, "You read to them. You're the mommy." Sarah replied, "But you're the mommy. I'm not the mommy." Sarah expressed an elaborated denial, using the variant form *but Y not X*, but she did not understand (or was not willing to accept) her mother's pretend orientation. Children must learn that the judgment, true or false, must also take into account the domain within which that judgment can appropriately be made. Speakers must agree on whether their messages are to be judged against the conditions of the literal world or the conditions of an imaginary or hypothetical one.

A very early use (or abuse) of the concept of true and false is the intentional misnaming of objects when the child knows the correct name. Such responses pose a problem for the researcher who wishes to assess a child's understanding of the different negative and positive relations, but they are a common form of humor in early childhood. A two-year-old finds it highly amusing to point to a ball and assert, "This is a garden," as one of Roy Pea's children did, or to announce, as Judy (32 months) did to her friend Tom, "I'm a big boy." Such responses suggest an understanding that predictions can either correspond or not correspond to facts in the conventional world. A next step is to understand that if the relevant persons agree, some facts may be accepted as true, say, in a pretend world or a play world, while being patently false in the conventional world. This is an understanding that Sarah's older friend Becky (37 months) seems to have attained, while Sarah at 29 months was still denying certain pretend facts in favor of the literal, or conventional, judgment, as the following example illustrates. Sarah was watching Becky drive off on the large wooden car. Becky was making *beep-beep* noises.

Sarah	Becky
	Get out of the road, all right?
What road?↘	
	The one I'm driving in. There's a lot of traffic in here. I'm driving on my car.
No, this is . . . no, this is a rug. (*Looks down at the carpet.*)	
	No, it's a road. Want to feel it? Feel. Feel with your hand, all right?

The ability to use truth-functional negation appropriately, then, depends on more than the ability to examine a situation and match an appropriate statement to it; it also depends on the context in which the judgment is understood.

Another development in the use of truth-functional negation reflects the broad, general advance toward cognitive decentration. The topics of negation expand from events and objects in the present and in the immediate environment or matters concerning the child's immediate actions or desires to events in the past and future and to ones more distant from the child's actions or sensations. This development makes it possible to discuss differing views of past events, to anticipate negative states of affairs, and to generalize about recurrent events. For example, Judy (32 months) and Tom (33 months) were discussing what they would do after the play session.

Tom said, "When we go to McDonald's, you'll get a hot dog." Judy replied, "No, we don't get hot dogs at McDonald's, we just get hamburgers instead." She used the logical pattern *not X because Z; but Y* in denying a prediction of a future event, giving the reason for the denial, and stating the correct positive case.

As children become more aware of other people's beliefs and perceptions, they can take these into account in denying not only what another person has said, but what that person may assume or expect. They can deny or correct a presupposition of another person's message. For example, when Tom (32 months) handed Judy (31 months) a small toy and asked, "How does this open?" she correctly replied, "It doesn't open. It just clicks." She explicitly corrected the presupposition of Tom's question, that the toy opened, and also informed him of the correct, positive state of affairs. The contrast between the two facts was marked by the word *just*. Along with the logical connectives, the subtle adverbs and particles, *just*, *only*, and *instead*, contribute to marking the relations between positive and negative messages in elaborated denials and corrections.

VERBAL CONFLICTS

The development of the meanings of negation is intricately related to advances in cognition, to increasing linguistic capabilities, to changes in affective and interpersonal adaptations, and to the differentiation of social activity in early and later childhood. One of the arenas for developing negation is in the speech events called quarrels, arguments, and verbal conflicts. Such events are not, of course, limited to moves that contain negative forms; opposition rather than negation defines these events. We can now examine how verbal conflicts arise, how they are conducted, and how they terminate.

Conflicts of interest are a fact of life in children's interactions. The vast majority of toddlers' clashes arise over the issue of possession or use of objects; such problems have been observed to occur as frequently as eleven or twelve per hour in small day care or nursery groups. The struggles, which are brief, often escalate rapidly to loud protest, screams, or crying and are terminated by the intervention of a teacher or parent. Even at that age, however, the success of an attempt to take an object and the probability that such an attempt will be resisted are influenced by the primitive understanding of a basic social rule: the right of prior possession.[8] (As was described in Chapter 4, this rule also plays an important part in the use of requests for permission.)

Parents and teachers urge contentious two-year-olds to take turns with objects and to substitute words for physical struggles. In the third year of life not only do children begin to resolve conflicts by talking, but by then they have already learned to create conflicts by talking as well. Quarrels and verbal aggression increase between the ages of two and four (as does all verbal activity), and new offensive techniques such as name-calling and teasing are added to the repertoire. Real proficiency in personal disparagement increases through adolescence, as do the abilities required for persuasion and for conflict resolution. Developmentalists have been particularly interested in the changes that take place in the form of verbal conflicts during early and middle childhood. While such conflicts decrease in frequency over this period, they become more complex, involve a greater variety of issues, and employ more flexible strategies.

Rational argumentation is the exchange of divergent

views supported by evidence acceptable to both parties. Its ideal outcome is compromise or reconciliation of the opposing views or acceptance of one of the positions as superior on some valued dimension such as accuracy, accountability, or reasonableness. The quarrels of young children rarely measure up to this ideal. Piaget characterized the clashes of children as exchanges of opinions or conflicting desires. The opinions and desires are not rationally supported; during the period of cognitive centration children do not understand others' different viewpoints and do not comprehend the logical relations of assertion and supporting evidence. Children later produce primitive arguments in which they take turns setting forth divergent opinions but still fail to support those positions rationally. The mature forms and processes of genuine argument are achieved later, facilitated, Piaget believed, by the experiences of interactions in which children attempt to coordinate their activities. In the process they learn that others can indeed hold different views, which can be compared and evaluated. Piaget maintained that equality of status promotes the comparison of divergent viewpoints and motives and leads the child not only to intellectual cooperation with others but to increased understanding of himself as well.[9] No direct comparisons have been made, however, between the verbal conflicts of peers and those between children and adults to examine the influence of equal and unequal status on the form or content of confrontations. It is true that many disagreements do arise (and many are resolved) in the course of otherwise collaborative activity such as pretend play. Also young children engage each other in explicit interchanges of reciprocal comparison of ages, size, families, experiences, and abilities, showing considerable interest in their similarities and differences.

Several studies have examined the verbal conflicts of peers,[10] and detailed observations of children's verbal interactions at home, school, or in play groups inevitably provide numerous instances of conflicts. Even children as young as two and a half years engage in a variety of verbal conflicts. Perhaps the earliest recorded instance of a contradiction, a conflict of predictions, was from a pair of Yugoslav twins who at 17 months argued about whether their uncle would come to visit them with his daughter Minja.[11] In translation:

Twin A	Twin B
Uncle come.	
	No, uncle not come.
Minja come.	
	No, Uncle-Minja not come.
Again, Uncle-Minja come.	
	Not again.

This argument is built up from the basic exchange type, assertion and denial, and uses a pattern of repetition of that exchange type. This is a basic framework for verbal conflicts throughout the ontogeny of this type of verbal interaction. A number of other techniques, however, are soon added to children's repertoire for oppositions.

The previous examples of truth-functional negation contained attempts to justify discordant positions with elaborated denials. Three-year-olds have learned to demand and to supply supporting evidence for conflicting assertions and are beginning to use strategies for refusing requests that supply "reasons" for noncompliance, although those reasons are usually self-referenced, for example, "No, because I'm using it." Whether they are able to resolve a conflict of interest depends, however, on a number of factors, including the availability of an adult to whom they can appeal for support, the presence of other children, and the strength of their personal interest, as when the issue involves a favorite toy. It is probably important for children to try to resolve conflicts themselves, to learn what techniques and strategies are effective in persuading another to share a toy or activity, and to accept a plan for joint action. An unresolved conflict terminates an engagement, at least temporarily, but a resolution permits continued play and collaboration. That children learn this during the preschool years is indicated by the finding that verbal conflicts are increasingly embedded in ongoing interactions. While the ideal of rational argumentation is realized only in later years, preschoolers are already practicing techniques for conflict resolution. They have learned certain ways of expressing opposition and of meeting opposition that are effective in the peer group. One secret of success seems to be the rule: take into account what your partner *says*.

In a study of the verbal conflicts of eighty-eight same-aged pairs of preschool children ranging in age from 34 months to 67 months, Ann Eisenberg and I examined all instances in which one child verbally opposed a partner's action or message during a fifteen-minute interaction session.[12] In all, there were 221 episodes. The episodes were easily identified: we located the verbal opposition, tracked back to the prior message or action that it addressed, and moved forward to the point at which a resolution was achieved or the conflict was abandoned. (The children were alone in the observation/playroom with no adult to intervene in the conflict.) We found that it was not possible to predict in advance how a conflict would begin. Almost any remark could be challenged, and even a seemingly innocuous suggestion or request could be opposed. (Negative answers to *yes/no* questions were not counted as oppositions, because the person who has framed a request for information in that way has given the addressee the option of a negative reply.) Although 57 percent of the conflicts concerned objects or actions, pretend identities or plans were also debated. Facts, opinions, or beliefs accounted for only 12 percent of the disputes.

The opposition, or negating response, creates two interpersonal roles, those of the opposer and the opposee. The two children act in those roles throughout the adversative episode. Although the messages used in the two roles may be similar in linguistic structure, such as the assertion, "I'm going to drive the car," the functional significance of the moves realized by those messages is different; if made by the opposee, the assertion is a claim, but if the opposer engages his partner in the conflict, it is a counterclaim. We found that initial opposing moves were most often formulated in one of five ways. To a claim such as "I'm going to drive the car," an opposition could be: 1) a simple negative response, "No," or the equivalent, "No, you're not"; 2) a reason for opposing, with or without an explicit negative, "No, it's mine" or "It's mine"; 3) a counterproposal or substitution, with or without a negative, "You ride on the tractor"; 4) a postponement of compliance or agreement, "Later you can"; or 5) an evasion or hedge, "It's not a car; it's a truck." Types 4 and 5 were relatively infrequent; type 2 was by far the most common in initial oppositions. If the move was a simple negative, as were 35 percent of all initial opposing moves, the episode was very likely to continue. Opposees did not simply accept a simple negative response and abandon the topic. If the initial opposition included a reason or countering move, however, the episode was far more likely to be terminated. That is, the children more often accepted an opposition if it was accompanied by some additional information. They seemed to expect the same kind of accounting that ritual considerations demand in more mature oppositional conduct. For adults, at least, the rule is: In refusing, disagreeing, or contradicting, don't just say "no"; provide an account.

For those episodes that continued after the initial opposition, there were eight major categories of subsequent moves employed by both adversaries. Some moves were successful in terminating the episode; that is, either the conflict was abandoned, or one of the two accepted the other's position. Other moves tended to prolong the conflict or led to blows or a huff. In the following descriptions of these moves, the percentages that led to successful termination of the conflict are indicated in parentheses.

1. Compromise (77 percent). Some kind of sharing or turn-taking is proposed. For example, after the opposer had objected to the opposee's plan to drive the car, the opposee suggested, "We can take turns driving the car."
2. Condition (53 percent). Compliance or agreement is promised if some other condition is met. For example, if the opposee continued to insist on driving the car, the opposer might say, "I'll let you drive the car if you'll drive me to Grandmother's."
3. Counter (40 percent). An alternative plan or a substitute is proposed. The opposee might counter the objection by saying, "You play with this snake."
4. Reason (34 percent). The opposee attempts to justify or explain his position. He might reply, "Yes, I have to drive the car 'cause I have to go to work."
5. Request for explanation. This move did not terminate

an episode, but 85 percent of such requests were met by a move that supplied a reason, explanation, or justification.

6. Mitigation or aggravation (13 percent). No new material is provided, but the child's previously stated position is either softened by adding *please* or by changing to a more polite paraphrase *or* it is intensified by increased loudness or changed from a request to a direct command. For example, the opposee might mitigate his claim by saying, "I'm going to drive the car. Please," and the opposer might aggravate his opposition by shouting, "You are not."

7. Insistence (13 percent). Either child simply repeats his own prior message, reinforces it with a simple "no" or "yes," or substitutes a simple "no" or "yes" for the message.

8. Ignoring. The partner's position is not acknowledged, perhaps because it was not heard or not understood, but perhaps because it is willfully ignored.

Three infrequent types of moves (twelve or fewer instances) were rarely successful in terminating an episode. These were use of physical force (grabbing, shoving, hitting); postponing or temporizing; and evading. One other type of move, a threat, was rare among these children, but has been observed by other researchers; "I will hit you" or "I will tell on you."

We believe that the first four move types listed above were most successful because they provided the partner with more than simple opposition. Each type represents some attempt at adapting to the other person's needs or interests. The most successful move, compromise, presents the clearest concession to the other person's desire or opinion while still permitting the speaker to retain, at least in part, his initial position. Moves 1 to 7 are listed in order of decreasing adaptiveness, insistence being the least adaptive because it makes no attempt to adapt.

Can children, in their everyday interactions with peers, learn the kind of practical social reasoning that the successful moves represent? Can they also discover what doesn't work? To answer these questions we analyzed sequences of moves in the episodes. Several patterns revealed that a child's subsequent move was influenced by the partner's prior move. Moves did not follow one another randomly; instead, one type of move was highly likely to be followed by a specific type of response. Several of the patterns of move sequences were so regular that a child could well derive the following practical rules from experiences of conflict with peers:

1. Insistence leads the partner to insist also.
2. Ignoring the partner's message is most likely to result in the partner rephrasing that message.
3. A move that offers compromise, a counterproposal, or even a condition for accepting the partner's position is likely to lead the partner to end the conflict.
4. Supplying a reason for one's position is likely to lead to a conciliatory move and is not likely to lead to a rigid or inflexible response.

Not only was the type of move contingent on the prior move, but the semantic content of the partner's message was often used in framing the response to it. Even while continuing to oppose, a child would use the material provided by the partner's response. Thus while still in a state of conflict, the children collaborated in shaping their verbal responses to acknowledge the partner's formulations of a reason, a postponement, or countering statement. This gradual rapprochement of verbal expression seemed to provide a path to resolving the conflicting positions. For example, if the opposer evaded the request, "Can I ride on the car?" by replying, "It's not a car. It's a truck," and the opposee countered by saying, "I know. Can I ride on the truck?" the opposition has been weakened, and the opposer pressured either to consent or to invent a more effective means of opposition. We subsequently observed a similar strategy, which might be described as "accept the words but persist in one's position" used by two-year-old friends. Tom at 33 months wanted to ride on the wooden car that Judy (32 months) was playing with. She was spinning the wheel around and Tom was watching.

Tom	Judy
What you doin'?	
	I'm spinning this around.
Can I see it?	
	No, not for a couple of months ago, 'cause I wanna see it right now. I have to see it first.
After you're done, I see it? ↗	
	(*Continues spinning the wheel.*) And then you can spin it around with your hand. Like this. (*Does it again.*)
Now can I do it?	
	No. Yes, have to push in the beep thing when this green light stops. (*Pushes on the horn.*)

When it stops I can do
it? ↗

> When the green lights
> comes, you know what
> I'm gonna drive to
> McDonalds . . . (*Continues*
> *with long account of what she*
> *will buy at McDonalds.*)

It would be nice to be able to report that after issuing the series of verbally accommodative rerequests, Tom finally got to play with the car, but he did not. He was forced to abandon the attempt as Judy, continuing to talk, drove off to McDonald's. However, Judy's temporizing responses, which took some account of Tom's formulations, may have helped to avoid a more unpleasant outcome. Whether her behavior was actually strategic or not, Tom did shape his rerequests to incorporate material from her messages, as in his last request, which accepts the time when the (imaginary) green light stops as a possible point when he might get to spin the wheel.

Linguistic cooperation is even more pronounced in the content and style of conflicts among older children. Pairs of primary school children from white and black American communities and pairs of Fiji Indian children were asked to role-play two types of conflicts. In one they were to pretend to quarrel about the use of an object; in the other, about which person was either stronger or smarter.[13] The children would match or build on one another's style tactics, responding in utterances of similar length, and each was influenced by the other's speed of speech, loudness, or stress pattern. They would also build on one another's imagery in making fantastic claims and counterclaims. For example, in one sequence the following turns show a stepwise escalation of the content of the prior message, each child incorporating the partner's material and extending it. *A:* "I can lift up this whole school." *B:* "I can lift up our whole family. I bet you can't lift up that with one finger." *A:* "I can lift up the whole world with one finger." *B:* "Well, I can lift up the universe." Since the children were pretending to have a quarrel, their productions were more highly stylized than are most genuine confrontations. The regularity of the patterning of exchange and exchange sequences reported in these studies, however, shows that the participants understood the underlying structure of verbal conflict. That competence can be used to enact a conflict within the pretend frame or in a more seriously motivated confrontation.

Resolution of divergent views or desires is not always the primary goal in verbal conflicts. Children also engage in special types of verbal conflicts that are shaped by other objectives. In some social groups certain modes of verbal aggression are valued as an index of individual skill, and in some cases might even be counted as an art form; a virtuoso performance is admired. In a Hawaiian neighborhood Karen Watson-Gegeo and Stephan Boggs observed joking, teasing, and the more complex talk story.[14] The latter was a narrativelike speech event produced collaboratively by two or more children; the story, or gag, unfolded as the speakers competed, contradicted, teased, challenged, and insulted one another and even brought the appreciative audience into the play. Underlying these social productions was a basic type of exchange sequence called the "contradicting routine"; one person denied the claim, challenge, or accusation of the other. Parents modeled and elicited playful contradictions with the children and encouraged their attempts. Children used the contradicting routine in their disputes, and older children skillfully incorporated it into the longer and more complex productions of sexual teasing and talk stories, which were a popular form of entertainment.

The ability to stand up for oneself, to counter teasing, and to defend oneself by verbal counterattacks or to put down an opponent by wit is highly valued in many social groups. Where this is the case, children must learn these skills either from other children or from adults, who may encourage the children to learn the basic forms of oppositional repartee. Peggy Miller encountered a total of twenty teasing sequences in six hours of video recordings of a mother and her two-year-old daughter from a lower socioeconomic, white urban community. The mother would issue a mock challenge, insult, or threat, saying in a special, taunting tone of voice, "You can't have that baby," while taking away the child's doll, and then would encourage her daughter to make a spirited response. Over a period of several months the child became more adept at recognizing the cues that signaled the teasing and at responding to or even initiating such mock disputes herself.[15] To take part in these bouts, which the mother considered important training in self-reliance and self-defense, the child had to learn the verbal formulas of initiation and response, the vocal cues that marked the teasing orientation (as distinct, say, from a seriously intended prohibition or refusal), and the facial expressions and physical gestures that together identified and constituted this type of interaction. The teasing bouts, Miller pointed out, were a part of the language socialization in this household and, one would expect, in the family's community as well.

More than communicative skill is required for successful verbal aggression and for defense against it. Not only do the techniques of persuasion in the face of refusal require the opposee to adapt his arguments to the opposor's interests; the techniques for injuring another verbally also require a knowledge of the intended victim. The topic of the verbal aggression must be of intense personal concern, perhaps a valued possession, relationship, personal attribute, or ability. An effective threat or insult embodies accurate knowledge of the opponent's desires and weaknesses as well as knowledge of the values and norms of the group to which the contestants belong. Personal insults and other techniques for attacking the self-esteem of others grow more common and more accurately targeted among older children and adolescents; preschoolers rarely engage in this type of verbal aggression. The point has been made that "developing is not always improving," and this is particularly true of the ability to perceive and attack another person's vulnerability. The abilities needed to select a hurtful accusation or to deny it and inflict even greater damage with words require knowing "what the other is like" and understanding operations of more mature social cognition.

In summary, the basic meanings of negation are differentiated during the first two to three years of life. These meanings express attitudes of resistance/refusal/prohibition; the experiences of disappearance/termination/reversal of expectation/failure; and finally, the relations of truth and falsehood in contradicting denials. The meanings are intimately associated with contrasting positive meanings and come to be elaborated, often explicitly, with explanations, justifications, and affirmations related to the negative message. Opposition to the desires, opinions, or expectations of others uses the basic meanings to accomplish a number of interpersonal aims.

Both cognitive and linguistic growth support the development of verbal conflicts. The aims of adversative interactions range from getting or retaining an object, to supporting a reasoned argument, to such primarily aggressive goals as personal injury or domination. These aims shape the selection of strategies, but in the conflicts of very young children, where the goal is most often getting one's own way with an object, activity, or plan, some type of adaptation to the position of the opponent proves to be a practical and effective strategy. As with all social activities, both the aims and strategies of interpersonal conflict are differentially supported by the family and the community group to which the child belongs.

Two friends in the playroom prepare for pretend play. Anne (35 months) speaks on the toy telephone, and Jack (33 months) watches her.

Anne	Jack
Hello . . . Bye (*on telephone*).	
	Who was that?
That was daddy.	
	What? ↗
That was daddy.	
	Daddy?
Let's go for walk with daddy. Let's pretend /	
	Okay, let's pretend.
Let's pretend.	
	I will bring this . . . with me. (*Picks up broom.*) And this. (*Picks up pocketbook.*)
That's mine. Mine. (*Takes the pocketbook from him.*)	
	And I'll carry this. (*Picks up Raggedy Ann doll.*) Will you/ I will carry this dolly.
I'm gonna take a broom. (*Picks up broom Jack has dropped.*)	
	Where's daddy?
He's over here. (*Turns and points to other side of room.*) Okay?	
	Okay.
Have to go pee.	
	Who/ who has to go pee-pee? ↗
Me. We have to go see daddy.	

6 / The Social Life

For children from the age of two on, talk becomes more and more central to the increasingly diverse events and transactions of life. In this chapter I will examine some of the ways in which talk serves the important social goals of initiating and constructing such focused engagements as teaching, trading, and playing; its role in shaping and organizing children's group activities; and its contributions to friendships. In some transactions talk appears to be primarily instrumental in achieving some immediate end, such as persuading another to return a purloined object, getting help in completing a puzzle, or gaining admittance to an ongoing group activity. At other, less urgent, times talk may be an end in itself, joined just for fun or for its intrinsic interest. An observer might postulate that the "conversationalists" have an urge to affiliate, but the children may be simply exploring the discovery that engaging another person in talk is in some ways more pleasurable and exciting than talking without a partner. But whatever the immediate motive or effect, social talk becomes a part of each child's developing style of interpersonal behavior. Recurring patterns of verbal interaction, along with nonverbal communication, come to constitute the somewhat more lasting complexes of attitudes, expectations, and interdependencies between persons that we think of as relationships. Before we ex-

155

amine the important transactions in which talk plays a central role, I will describe some of the characteristics of "just conversing."

JUST CONVERSING

What is a conversation? It proves easier to say what a conversation is not than to define it by its attributes.[1] We do not consider business transactions or any interchange having planned procedures or previously stated goals, such as solving a problem, teaching a skill, or disciplining another person, as conversational. The term is usually reserved for informal, more or less spontaneous interchanges in which a few or just two persons alternately introduce and jointly pursue topics in a leisurely manner without an explicitly prearranged agenda. A conversation can be embedded in some other type of interaction or can constitute a whole encounter. When do children begin to converse in this sense? Certainly conversations occur during the preschool period, both with adults and with other children. Conversations thrive in familiar settings and with familiar persons, especially between pairs, since handling the necessarily responsive contributions of conversation is difficult with more than one partner at a time.

Young children, at least when they are well and at ease, are usually busily pursuing some line of action or are in momentary transition from one project to another. Much of a child's talk arises from and accompanies his own activities, and if two or more children are in physical proximity, the talk functions rather like a radio device that permits each to monitor where the action is and to "home in" on it if it seems interesting. A three-year-old typically either invites another to join or attend to his own activity, "Look what I'm making," or displays his involvement both verbally and nonverbally so that a monitoring partner is drawn in and action can become coordinated, at least for a brief period before some distraction or new project begins. Making one's action intelligible to another is a problem of some magnitude to very young children; if one is to join the other's action, it is critical to determine what the other is doing. Understanding what is going on proves to be essential for a slightly older child who wants to enter into the ongoing activities of a group of mutually involved children, as we shall see in a subsequent section of this chapter. But even in the pairs of young friends we studied, the question, "What you doin'?" was often addressed to one child by another and rarely failed to bring forth an action-defining formulation, such as "Making coffee." A little less frequently both children together would construct a joint line of action and pursue it together, beginning, perhaps, with a "let's" suggestion, or by jumping directly into a coordinated activity.

In her several studies of the way action lines converge among pairs of children, Grace Wales Shugar found that three-year-olds joined a partner's action line less often than they drew a partner into their own line of action; four-year-olds joined a partner's line more frequently and were also more likely than the younger children to jointly initiate coordinated action. (In contrast, in the children's interactions with an adult, the adult tended to join the child's action line.) In this flow of converging, dissolving, and again converging action, brief conversations begin to appear between familiar and friendly children. Although they may emerge out of a shared action line, these episodes of "topical discourse" become, as Shugar says, dislodged from the immediate action.[2] They are instances of just conversing. The topics may be selected from memories, may be plans for the near future, or may express opinions or emotions. They display a reciprocity of attention and concern, regardless of the topic, although they are not always as harmonious as the following conversation between Judy (32 months) and Tom (33 months), who at this point in their play session were not sharing any line of action except the verbal focus created in talk. In this example Tom abandoned his action line and proposed a topic to join the topical focus that Judy introduced:

Tom	Judy
(*Sits on the wooden car.*) I'm the driver (*explaining his own action line*).	(*Stands beside the car.*)
	I'm tired (*introducing her self-reporting topic*).
Why?↘ Would you like a square dice? (*referring to a plastic block*).	
	No, thank you. I'm not sick.
They make you better. Do you want one? They make you better. (*Holds it out to her.*)	
	No, I don't want any.
All right.	I'm not sick anymore.
Are you sick?	
	No.
I'm not either. I'm not sick either.	
	(*Judy abandons the topic and tells Tom to turn off the car.*)

In a rather more mature-sounding conversation, a five-year-old boy and girl alternately contributed opinions concerning their time in the playroom. The topic was embedded in a pretend play sequence (both children were sitting on the car) but was quite independent of it, and both lowered their voices during this exchange of views:

Boy	Girl
(*Makes driving noises.*)	
	I think we're gonna be picked up soon, don't you?
Hey, I think they're gonna come over now. (*Turns head to listen.*) I hear someone walking. (*He is hearing steps in the hall.*)	
	(*Gets off car, goes to door, looks out, then back to partner.*) I think I hear them, don't you?
I don't think it's for us (*as sound of steps passes*).	
	We just came in here, right?
Yeah.	
	I think it's juice and cookies time, don't you? (*She may be referring to that time at nursery school.*)
No, it wouldn't be.	
	(*Play resumes.*)

Neither of the above conversations exhibited a playful orientation, but many conversational episodes do; playful teasing, contributions that are meant and are taken to be funny, and topics from the realm of fantasy were common in most of the pairs we observed. Indeed, Anca

Nemoianu has used the term "conversation-play" to characterize the talk during social interaction of three children she observed over a six-month period, maintaining that it is often difficult to distinguish the boundaries of and transitions between playful and nonplayful attitudes in the flow of activity.[3] In many cases this is true, although role play, as we will see in Chapter 7, does employ distinctive verbal markers to identify portrayed characters. One variety of play interchange, however, is distinctly different from other kinds of talk and must be mentioned here, since it has been suggested as one of the precursors of conversational exchange among peers.[4] That is socially constructed sound play, so called because the content comprises sounds or nonsense words. In such episodes turns are alternated promptly and rhythmically, but each child successively repeats and/or slightly modifies the form, rather than the content, of the previous turn. In similarly rhythmic, but referentially interpretable verbal play episodes, it is still the form more than the content, or meaning, that makes the episode cohesive, with each child building on the other's turn by repetition and some limited modification or expansion of the prior turns. In the same session in which Judy and Tom produced the conversational episode cited earlier, they also produced the following rhythmic and playful episode in which repetition and successive modification were the organizing principles. Tom began by picking up a word from Judy's prior utterance (they had been talking about where the parents of Judy's baby doll were).

Judy	Tom
Well, someday you can see the dada, but not for a long time.	
	I have a dada, too.

I have a dada, too.

     I have a *real* dada.

I have a special dada.

     I have a real dada.

I do too.

     I do too.

I have a special dada, too.

     I do too.

I have a special dada doo.
Da daaa. (*Starts to chant.*)

Among preschool children such markedly playful episodes coexist with more "serious" interchanges and with
those that consist of dramatic or fantasy play.[5] Although
episodes of sound play become less frequent, these ritualized play patterns do continue to occur and seem to
have a communicative function and special form of their
own.[6] As such, they are not a likely preparation for just
conversing. Further, sound play and ritualized verbal
play are rarely observed in interactions between caregiver
and child when the child is beginning his conversational
life, although just conversing on a topic, usually one introduced by the child himself, often occurs in the inter-
stices of more task-oriented talk with the caregiver. Just
conversing, then, is one social activity that increases in
frequency and in diversity of topic over the preschool
years to become an important type of sharing among
children and a major constituent of the interactions of
most close friends, both displaying and reinforcing solidarity and intimacy.

BREAKING AND ENTERING

A child brought into a new situation, such as a new-
comer to an established nursery school class, tends to

speak very little at first; he behaves unobtrusively and spends his time watching the habitués. His first overtures are likely to be tentative. (Even a pair of children who do not know each other usually begin their interaction cautiously, with "getting acquainted" moves such as asking for the other's name.) Saying the right thing in the right way is one important step in initiating the interactions that will lead to acceptance and in avoiding ones that will lead to ever-worsening relations. When several children are together, in a day care center, at a birthday party, play group, or school, groupings inevitably appear. Some clusters may form voluntarily during a free period; some are engineered by an adult for routine activities, such as making valentines, working on an assignment, or having a snack. In voluntarily formed groups, particularly, and in those where adult supervision or direction is minimal, the basis of the temporary cohesion is likely to be a shared activity to which the members are committed. Members form a "we" and are protective of their psychological and physical interactive space and possessive of the objects involved in their mutually defined activity. Entering such a group (and such a group can appear powerfully attractive to a solitary child or one who is in transition from one involvement to another) poses a serious problem, not only to the socially inept or relatively unpopular child, but even to the more socially skilled and popular child. Members of a group will often react quite fiercely to the outsider's first bid for entry. In fact, in nursery school groups of both three- and four-year-old children who had been together in the classes for several months and thus were acquainted with each other, half of all first entry bids were rejected by the involved group. Typical rejection moves were "Go away" and "You can't play," followed by such reinforced rejections as "We don't like you today" and "You're not our friend."[7] Knowing that such a reaction is likely, the outsider, not surprisingly, generally approaches the group with some trepidation, watching and hesitating before first attempting to join. He also realizes that he must be ready to persist in his attempts when he is either ignored or rebuffed.

A number of factors influence the probability of gaining access to a group. One is the perennial sex problem. A girl's chances of joining a group of boys are fairly poor. The group's rationale for exclusion is often quite straightforward. For example, a girl ran up to two boys on a swing and asked, "Can I get on?" Each boy forcibly replied, "No," and one boy went on to tell her, "We don't want you on here. We only want boys on here."[8] Another factor is the stability and solidarity of the group itself. If it is composed of close friends, who are probably engaged in established and jointly evolved play activities, the outsider has little chance of being accepted. The intimate group has its own language of friendship and familiar interaction patterns. Catherine Emihovich observed three very close four-year-old friends in a nursery school class of fourteen children for a period of four months. At the beginning of the semester the friends were the only children who called one another by name, and they regularly played a domestic scenario together, each taking the same pretend roles on each occasion. They resisted entry bids from other children, and after a few sessions the other children in the class ceased trying to join their pretend play activities, although one girl did become a friend of the girl in the established group and was subsequently admitted to play a role in the "family," which was expanded to accommodate her.[9]

The popularity of the outsider and the popularity of the children in the temporary activity groupings in a classroom or on the playground also influence the length of time a child watches, or "hovers," on the periphery of a group before attempting to gain admittance; the number of entry bids he may have to make before finally being admitted; and the likelihood that he will eventually succeed. Popularity is strongly tied to the communicative and interpretative skills required for successful entry into and functioning in a group. In the later preschool and early elementary school period children distinguish between acquaintances and strangers, and they also categorize other children as liked, or popular, or as unpopular, and thus generally less desirable as playmates. Popular children require less time and fewer entry bids to gain access to an activity group, especially when that group is composed of popular children. It is a bit more difficult for them to enter groups composed of unpopular children. Unpopular children, as might be expected, have a very hard time joining a group of popular children but manage a little better in joining other unpopular children (although still not as efficiently and successfully as popular children entering a more favored group). One secret of the popular children's success lies in their ability, displayed both verbally and nonverbally, to understand the structuring of the group's activities, to recognize what is going on, and to produce well-timed entry bids that accommodate to the group's involvement, thus minimizing any disturbance of the ongoing action. They have learned, in effect, the following guidelines. The Don't's: don't ask questions for information (if you can't tell what's going on, you shouldn't be bothering those who do); don't mention yourself or state your feelings about the group or its activity (they're not interested at the moment); don't disagree or criticize the proceedings (you have no right to do so, since you're an outsider).

The Do's: be sure you understand the group's frame of reference, or focus (are they playing house?); understand the participation structure of the activity; slip into the ongoing activity by making some relevant comment or begin to act in concert with the others as if you actually were a knowledgeable member of the group; hold off on making suggestions or attempting to redirect until you are well into the group.[10]

Because of the normally strong urge to be included, a child usually tries again after being rejected or simply ignored. Of course, a child can simply repeat his first attempt, a tactic more common among five-year-olds than seven-year-olds. But even preschoolers have some techniques for revising the bid, making it either more forceful or more ingratiating. Five-year-old girls tend to be a bit more flexible than boys in this respect, especially when their motive appears to be to gain entry to the group rather than to perform the activity itself or use the objects or props that the group commands. David Forbes and his colleagues, in their study of "third-party entry" among small groups of five- and seven-year-olds, have pointed out that these two types of motives, which often can be distinguished by the entering child's subsequent behavior in the group, influence the tactics used in attempting access.[11] A second or third entry bid is likely to be met with more elaborated resistance that rationalizes the rejection, a preferred basis being the prerogatives of the group. In defending the group against intruders, members emphasize their solidarity and their rights to control the group's resources. If the group is involved in pretend play, their make-believe roles are one basis for exclusion; for example, in repelling an intruder from some climbing bars, one boy said, "You can't get in [three times]. It's only for police. It's only for policemen." When the intruder left, the two playmates affirmed their togetherness: "Good. We got the run of *our* policehouse."[12] In such ways, members of a group display and reaffirm their mutual involvement, not only to outsiders but also to one another. After all, they share not only their physical proximity and a use space, but also the psychological sense of doing something together, something "we" have jointly created.

INSIDE A GROUP

The processes of mutual construction of an activity can be seen in the way temporary groupings of children negotiate just what it is they are doing, what procedural rules are in effect, how to delimit space, and how to allot materials, props, and the various responsibilities. In situations supervised or arranged by adults, the adult may impose a decision about some of these functions, as when a teacher organizes a group for collaborative work on a project or a parent suggests that playmates might like to have a tea party. But the organizational functions must be fulfilled and are undertaken by the children themselves whenever possible. Sometimes the process is democratic, sometimes one child emerges as the leader, whose suggestions and ideas are likely to be accepted, even solicited by the other members. In pretend play, many, if not all, of these organizational functions are verbalized, so I will focus on how they are accomplished in such play. In a later section of this chapter I will examine the communication within a group involved in teaching and other classroom tasks.

Several investigators have made very similar observations on the two types of communication required for pretend play in groups of two or more children. Dramatization is, of course, essential; the roles must be portrayed, and activities must be enacted. The other type of communication has been called explicit mention of pretend, framing statements, or negotiation.[13] Such communications are essentially metacommunicative; they are about the play and they serve the organizational functions listed above. The proportions of dramatization and negotiation about play differ, depending on the group. On any particular occasion a move directed at defining or organizing the activity may be accepted at once or may lead to a lengthy exchange sequence. The statements concerning various aspects of the group's activity need not occur in any prescribed order, although the assignment of person roles and the definition of the activity usually occur early in the interaction. The following are the major types of negotiable organizing statements, with an example of each (all bearing on the ubiquitous domestic theme):

Definition of situation: "Let's play house."

Assignment of roles: "I'll be the daddy and you be the mommy."—"And what will he be?" (indicating a third child)—"He's the little boy."

Defining location: "This is the kitchen."

Specifying the action plan: "I'll fix supper for the kid and you get the groceries."

Assigning props: "This is my pocketbook."

Correcting operating procedures and refining the script: "Daddies don't wear pocketbooks."—"My daddy wears pocketbooks."

Ku, .ing others' performance: "No, you have to really yell at him" (said by a girl when a boy playing Daddy did not speak sternly enough to the naughty "little boy").

Invoking rules relating to the real (versus the pretend) context: "You can't *really* go out there" (said by a girl when a boy actually started to open the door to the playroom on his pretend trip to the grocery store).

Termination of and/or transition from one organizing theme to another: "Okay, all finished supper."—"What do you want to play now?"
Commenting on the interpersonal climate in the group: "We're playing so we're friends now, right?"—"Right."

Talk is vital to the conduct of play. First, it defines and coordinates the participants' actions. Outsiders also, whether investigators or children hovering on the periphery of the group, poised to attempt entry, must listen in order to know what is going on. Imagine, for example, three children who could be objectively described as carrying boards to an enclosure of cardboard boxes. They could be transporting weapons to a fort, carrying beams to construct a roof for a new house, or lugging skis to a slope. Only their talk will reveal the import of their behavior. Second, the talk inside a group, in addition to organizing and dramatizing, serves the function of displaying and affirming membership, both to insiders and outsiders. The members often verbally mark their territory, reinforcing their consensus not only with references to *we* or *our house*, but also by repeating one another's verbal formulations. In the following example, two three-and-a-half-year-olds engaged in a building project repeated each other's phrases, acknowledged ("Yeah") and explicitly linked ("and") their messages.

Boy	*Boy*
There, we need a *lot more* tools.	
	We'll need a *lot* of tools.
Yeah, we might need a *lot* of them.	
	And we need a *lot* of screws.

These same children also used requests for permission in different ways depending on whether they were inside or outside a pretend engagement at that moment. As an outsider, a child would ask, "Can I try it?" and then wait for the response from the insiders who were working with some tool that was part of their pretend scenario (usually permission was not granted). The insiders, however, who had joint rights to their props, would ask permission of one another for a turn at using the prop but would not wait for a response. They would just begin the turn, having established a pattern of taking and relinquishing turns at using what belonged to both within the framework of the shared play theme.[14]

The domestic theme (illustrated in the above examples of negotiations) is the first to appear in young children's play and it is familiar to virtually all children. It can be endlessly varied and can be combined with other widely popular themes such as taking a vacation, surviving a disaster, and illness or injury followed by healing or recovery. If the children are well acquainted and imaginative, variations can become quite elaborate (the previous examples are relatively simple). The value children ascribe to such play and to good players and the fact that the play requires skilled negotiation and flexibility are two reasons that children who have friends are children who engage in more domestic fantasy play than relatively friendless children.[15]

BEING FRIENDS

The temporary groupings examined above provide the opportunity for interactions in which compatibility and mutual preferences can develop. Children who have friends are those who can get along with others. In the preschool period getting along means, first and foremost, playing together, taking turns at directing and being directed in play, and being able to defuse or resolve the inevitable disagreements and conflicts of interest that arise. But if friendship grows out of playing together, avoiding serious fights, and sharing things and activities (which is the definition of friendship that a preschooler will give, if asked), friendship itself is a relationship, a connection that extends beyond the actual interaction. Among three- and four-year-olds, the term "friend" usually refers to what they conceive of as friendly behavior, and it is often invoked for purposes of control, "I won't be your friend if you don't let me have a turn." But although young children may not yet consciously or explicitly conceptualize such an abstract idea as "relationship" or think about friends as loyal persons one trusts and admires, they exhibit attitudes toward one another that go beyond the momentary behaviors of compliance or cooperation. Friends want to be together, miss one another when they are apart, and share an intangible bond of memories, secrets, and understanding. In the late preschool period friends engage in fantasy play that reflects their (possibly otherwise inexpressible) concerns about being lonely, their fears and worries; and they are able to reassure one another. Having had more opportunity and greater motivation to understand one another's habits, moods, and preferences, they are better able to resolve misunderstandings and quarrels (and friends do quarrel), and are generally more responsive to each other than are children who are not friends.

Friends are able to construct together elaborate conspiracies, as John Gottman and Jennifer Parkhurst discovered in their study of good friends in their own homes. They identified a type of verbal interchange they dubbed "shared deviance," which involved planning naughty or forbidden acts, one lengthy example of which was a plot to poison the mother of one of the children by hiding some pretend lethal beans in a dish she was cooking. Mother was not poisoned, but the friends further consolidated their intimacy with the elaborate scheming.[16] In friendships favorite fantasy themes emerge and generally reach more imaginative and creative heights than in the fantasy play of less intimate children, most probably because the shared understandings and mutually constructed history of their play and life together permits the communicative work of play to move beyond the essential organizational negotiations into the exploration of both personal images and feelings and new experiences they want to share and extend.

TEACHING

Teaching and learning are achieved in a number of different ways; planned, explicit verbal instruction on a teacher-selected topic or task, as is common in classroom situations, is only one means by which children or adults transfer knowledge or skill to a young child. Much learning occurs outside of the settings of formal instruction as a child selects a procedure that interests him, watches and listens or asks a question, then recreates the procedure himself in his own way, often modifying his behavior in response to another's reactions. Those reactions include teasing, prompting, challenging, denigrating his ability, and ignoring certain inappropriate behaviors; these are all ways to shape a child's behavior and promote the learning of such disparate things as playing a jumprope game with the "right" counting-in and counting-out formulas, riding a bicycle, drying the dishes, or even reciting the alphabet. Very little is known about how children teach other children, or whether preschoolers intentionally set out to impart information or skill to a peer or "shape up" a peer's performance on a task. Children do imitate one another, and the preschool-age child is more likely to observe and imitate the behavior of a slightly older child than one his own age or size or a younger one. Children certainly do learn from one another, and in cultural groups in which siblings and other children assume part of the responsibility for child care, their influence may be of considerable importance. In our own culture, research on children's teaching has focused on the use of peer tutors in classroom situations, primarily during the later elementary school years.[17] In these situations "teaching" is likely to take on some characteristics of the explicit verbal instruction conducted by adult teachers. Before examining some of these more formal tutoring techniques, I will discuss some early forms of teaching and ask what three-year-olds know about this type of interpersonal engagement.

If we define teaching or instructing as one person's intentional attempt to convey information or skill he possesses (or believes he possesses) to a person who does not, then one can observe attempts at teaching by very young children. (Teaching and learning do not always go hand in hand, and I will not be primarily concerned with the success of these attempts.) One person sets himself forth as knowledgeable about an object or event or about how to do something, and the other attends to the explanation, instruction, or demonstration and tries to follow. Thus two reciprocal roles are established, one generally taken by an adult, the other by a child. Teaching episodes may be initiated either by the "teacher" or by the "pupil." The teacher may respond to a request or other indication of need, or the teacher, deciding that the pupil needs guidance in some ongoing activity, may initiate the teaching episode. Before examining the attempts at teaching that arise when two children take on the roles of teacher and pupil, I will briefly mention the far more familiar procedures of adult and child in an instructional engagement.

The caregivers of young children have an extensive repertoire of instructional techniques. Further, they generally have certain priorities and a changing agenda of topics for instruction. The mothers of the three two-year-olds, Judy, Jack, and Sarah, were all working on teaching, among many other things, numbers, colors, and animal names. These subjects were introduced, usually by the mothers, during play sessions and in a variety of other situations. The mothers all, for example, led the children to count things—eggs, forks, vegetables—and to name colors when they were working together in the kitchen, catching up on their teaching agendas on the fly and taking any other opportunity to explain such occasional topics as why yeast bread rises or why ice melts. More structured lessons on the continuing agendas were engineered during play with puzzles or blocks. In these situations the children entered easily into the pupil role, exhibiting their familiarity with the well-established, routinized exchange patterns. A typical example, between Jack (30 months) and his mother, engaged with a number puzzle, shows that Jack understood the procedure to the point where he could anticipate the next question. (Only the end of this long episode is presented.)

Jack	Mother
	What number is that? *(pointing to a piece Jack is holding)*.
One.	

Jack	Mother
	Good.
One.	
	And do you know what color it is? ↗
Yeah . . . Red.	
	Good.
It's red.	
	It's the same as this one (*pointing to another piece*). Same color. A different shape, but the same color. Now we have two left. (*Looks at Jack.*)
Greens.	
	Two greens. Very good.
What a / one, oh.	
	One, oh. That's right. And that's ten. (*Points.*) And that's four. (*Points at other piece.*)
Four. (*Puts "10" piece in puzzle.*) We're all finished with this.	
	Good job. Good job, Jack.

The dutiful pupil repeated his correct responses, which the teacher had praised; provided, unasked, the color and then the number name of one of the last two pieces (knowing, presumably, that he would be asked if he failed to volunteer the information); and put each piece into the puzzle after it had been identified. (The color red had been a particular issue during this session. During the next puzzle the pair worked with, Jack was unable to "show something else that's red" after his mother told him the color of an apple shape.) The format of the pedagogical "play" session with its clear differentiation of roles, the mother's elicitations (some masquerading as comments, "Now we have two left"), and the firmly maintained "on-task" orientation throughout the session will all be quite familiar and predictable to Jack when he encounters similar procedures for teaching in kindergarten and elementary school.

Did Jack and the other children ever reverse these roles and try to instruct their mothers? This happened in only one type of situation during the hours of interaction we recorded. Each child attempted to instruct his mother in how to take part in play events the child had devised. In these events, in which the child was, indeed, the knowledgeable party, the child explained his scenario, demonstrated actions, and told the mother what she should or should not do. In terms of instructional techniques, the children did not ask questions to check on the mother's understanding, did not praise her when she did something correctly, and did not even acknowledge her responses unless she asked for feedback, as in, "Is this the right way?" As a matter of fact, the mothers did not seem to play the pupil role any better than their children performed as teachers. They were overachievers, asking too many helpful questions and not refraining from making suggestions to make the activity more reasonable or intelligible or to bring it in line with their own agendas. Mothers' tendencies to shape play in this way have been observed to persist at least until the child is five years old.[18]

With little practice in the role of teacher, how does a child carry out this function when the pupil is another child? And how does a child perform as pupil vis-à-vis a peer, whom he may not see as a properly accredited teacher or even recognize as a teacher at all? Judy, Jack, and Sarah entered into only a few teaching episodes with their friends. The children did not have, after all, any long-range instructional agendas and had little expertise to impart. For the most part the episodes that did occur centered on how to do something. In the first instance of teaching we observed between Judy (29 months) and Tom (30 months), Tom asked Judy how to operate a little box that had two switches on it that activated a buzzer and some lights, which were shaped like buttons.

Tom (pupil)	*Judy (teacher)*
How does this turn on? How does this turn on, Judy?	
	(*Looks up at Tom from the baby doll she is caring for.*) Hafta . . . hafta push the little button.
(*Tries to push a button but gets no results.*) How's it go on?	
	(*Comes over to the box and explains but does not demonstrate.*) Hafta push your thumb. Hafta push with your finger, and then hafta stop it and everything like that.
(*Keeps trying.*)	
	(*Leaves Tom and box, no longer attending to his efforts.*)

In this instance Tom asked for help and Judy gave him (incorrect) instructions but took no further responsibility for showing him what to do. In the following instance, the roles of teacher and pupil were reversed, and Tom initiated the step-by-step instructions. This time the pupil followed each instruction, and the teacher demonstrated as well as told the pupil what actions would lead to success in "doing the wiper, too." Judy (31 months) had just gotten on the wooden car that Tom had been driving, and Tom (32 months) was standing beside it as she started to drive, turning the steering wheel:

Tom (teacher)	Judy (pupil)
And you do the wiper, too. (*Points to the gear shift lever.*)	
	(*Moves hand to lever.*)
You click it.	
	(*Tries to move lever.*)
No, this way. (*Reaches over and demonstrates by moving lever up and down.*) You do it like that. (*Withdraws his hand from lever.*)	
	(*She does move the lever several times.*)
And you push the / . . . beep the horn.	
	(*She pushes the inoperative horn, saying at the same time*) Beep. Beep, beep, beep.

In this instance the teacher attended to the pupil's response to the verbal instructions, reacted to her ineffectual attempt by adding a demonstration, then let the pupil do it herself. He did not go on to acknowledge her accomplishment but gave a new instruction relevant to driving the car. Judy accepted her male partner's automotive expertise.

The directive form exemplified by Tom's directions, "you push," "you click it," and "you do it," is often used, of course, in giving how-to-do-it instruction, and this form can also be used in teaching more general precepts, as can the *you have to* form. An example of giving a more general rule for behavior was the response by a four-year-old girl to her boy partner's announcement that when he grew up he was going to be a policeman. She said, "You have to be nice, then. Nice to nice people, then." This kind of teaching, which invokes norms of behavior, is quite rare among three-year-olds, but Anne (35 months) did instruct Jack (33 months) on a point of proper conduct after they had just discussed whether he had really soiled his diaper:

Anne (teacher)	*Jack (pupil)*
Sometimes you're play pooing on the potty.	
	Yes, and sometimes I go poop in my diaper.
No, you hafta go / . . . you hafta go poop in the bathroom. Big boys go in the potty. Allan stands up, and you stand up.	
	I sit down.

Anne tried to tell Jack about a conventional rule to guide his behavior and supported her position, citing general and specific authority, but whether Jack realized her attempt or not, we do not know.

From these fleeting instructional gestures to the beginnings of peer tutoring in the elementary classroom, we would expect the concepts of the reciprocal teacher–pupil roles to develop along with the appropriate verbal and nonverbal techniques and increased understanding of pupils' needs. Indeed, in studies of peer tutoring in which children have been taught to take the teacher role, part of the training involves focusing the tutee (usually a younger child) on the task, making the instructions clear and explicit, and giving prompt and helpful feedback on the tutee's efforts, all steps that are characteristic of mothers' (and other adult teachers') instructional procedures.[19]

Catherine Cooper and her colleagues have conducted a number of studies of both spontaneous teaching-learning engagements of children in relatively open classrooms where children are encouraged to work together and of situations in which children have been assigned the teacher role in an adult-specified task. In one second-grade classroom spontaneous engagements were initiated either by the learner or by the teacher. In both types the episodes far more often dealt with substantive issues, the spelling of a word or the answer to an arithmetic problem, than with procedural issues, such as, whether to cross out items on a page or circle them. Interestingly, the majority of episodes were initiated by the learner, and some children were chosen as teacher more frequently than others. These findings indicate that at least by the second grade, children do feel that they can gain information from other children and that they have some sense as to which child is able to provide it. Learner initiations varied in their directness, from explicit questions, "I still need help on number 3" or "The woman saw *what?*" to more indirect requests for help, "I don't get this right here" or "This one is hard for me," said while pointing to a task item. When children voluntarily assumed the role of teacher, they did not usually set up the task but began with an instruction or spontaneously corrected the pupil's work, "See the *d? d, b*" (pointing to each letter). "You were wrong." In one adult-assigned task a child who had been taught to use objects to balance a scale acted as teacher to a child pupil who was unfamiliar with the task. In this case Cooper found that the ability to give specific directions, both verbally and by gestural indication, was associated with successful teaching. In neither the teaching task nor in the classroom episodes did teachers consistently try to focus the pupils' attention, nor did they often give directive feedback, but when they did, these techniques were associated with successful interchanges.[20]

By second grade some children do display an understanding of the reciprocal responsibilities of the teacher and pupil roles. They know that the teacher must obtain the attention of a distracted or unwilling pupil, should confirm or otherwise indicate acceptance of a pupil's correct response, and correct an incorrect response or try again to elicit a correct one. John Gumperz and Eleanor Herasimchuk made a detailed comparison of the instructional episodes on reading of a second-grade child teacher and a first-grade pupil and those of the adult teacher with the children. The child teacher, they found, had to assert her role more forcefully to obtain initial cooperation on the task.

Child teacher	*Child pupil*
Come here. Sit down here.	
	Do you know any . . . like this? (*not referring to the reading task*).
Sit down here, *now.*	
	I don't want to read all them words.
Well, what's this word anyway?	
	I don't know.
Large.	
	What? ↗
Large.	
	Large.

Once engaged, the teacher and pupil collaborated in a way that contrasted markedly with that of the adult teacher and pupils. The child teacher used more direct elicitations and fewer indirect ones and hints than did the adult. The child teacher tended to model the correct response and to acknowledge the pupil's correct responses with repetitions. The adult teacher relied more on questions for elicitation and provided more explicit verbal feedback, "Right" or "That's good." A typical child–child sequence is the following:

Child teacher	*Child pupil*
They	
	They
Go	
	Go
They go down	
	They go down
To	
	To . . . the
Lunch	
	Lunch
Room.	

In this characteristic sequence the pupil reproduced not only the teacher's words but also the timing and intonation, which was the typical reading intonation, with individual words produced with level or low-rising pitch. The two children's contributions were balanced both in rhythm and in the actual number of words and utterances produced by each partner. The interchanges of the adult teacher and pupils were more asymmetrical; the teacher talked much more than the pupils, and her messages differed from theirs in form, content, and intonation.[21] While there is some evidence that children in the elementary grades can and do fulfill the reciprocal functions of the teacher and pupil roles and that the child teachers have acquired some techniques for focusing attention, maintaining an on-task orientation, and providing informative feedback, they must also adapt their practices to the child–child relationships that exist concurrently and, perhaps, more basically in their classroom or work group.

TRADING

Of the many social tasks the child encounters in his daily life that are constructed in part or in whole by talking, only a few have been described in detail. Trading is one type of well-motivated talk interchange that most children probably engage in, and Elliot Mishler has analyzed the bargaining of six-year-old boys, who can engage in this strategic and orderly activity with some skill. A lunch or snack packed by a well-meaning parent often provides the basic resources for trading, but marbles or other personal possessions may also be used, as long as the participants know the rules of the game. As in many other games that children play, the rules are probably learned from peers or siblings, and learning is most likely by observation and practice during the later preschool and early elementary school years.

The basic conditions for trading are that each party has a tradable object and a motive for exchange. Talk has a central role in the interchange from its outset. As Mishler puts it, "The problem for participants is to express the trading relevance of their own objects and motives, to assess the presence of similar relevances in others, and to elicit their expression from them." Tradable objects must differ in some way; if two children discover that they both have Snack Packs or the same kind of candy bar, no trading episode will result. The objects must be presented in such a way that their differences can be assessed for their trading value. In the two complementary roles, person *A* must not only exhibit his interest in a possible trade but must also present his object as desirable to person *B*. *B*, too, must entertain the idea of a trade and convey the value of his object. Both *A* and *B*, as the process unfolds, may enhance their bargaining positions by playing down their eagerness to have the other's object, perhaps by devaluing the object. Both parties must know that what they are doing is trading, rather than joking, perhaps, or offering the object as a gift or just arguing about whose possessions are better. An intelligible episode of trading comes into being in the exchange of sequenced moves.

The first move is a delicate one. The objects must be displayed, but the first person to make an explicit trading request is likely to be in the weaker position. The other party might refuse or try to strike a harder bargain if he sees the initiator as being eager for the trade. For example, an opening display, "I got a Suzy Q" (candy bar), was rebuffed by a potential trading partner, "That's not a Suzy Q," and the initiator was forced to argue that it was, indeed, what he claimed. He then selected another potential trading partner and tried again: "I got something interesting. Suzy Q's." He went on to make a trading bid: "What will you give me for a Suzy Q?"

The next step, if a partner is successfully engaged, is to refine the terms of the deal. Here the participants repeatedly advance and parry moves designed to gain an advantage. In one episode in which the resources were cookies and popcorn, a series of exchanges was devoted to arriving at mutually acceptable equivalence. *A:* "If I give you one of these, you gimme a whole hanful . . . cuz if I give ya just that/" *B:* "Look, I don't want a broken one." *A:* "Here. Yer supposta gimme a whole han*ful.*" *B:* "Gimme another cookie and I'll give ya . . ." Rules for equivalence are advanced and each can be debated: *B:* "Those are smaller. So if I give you one, you'd hafta give me like five." *A:* "You give me two and I'll give you 'bout this much."[22] Whether the arguments are logical or only ad hoc issues of personal preference, each must be answered in turn if the episode is to continue to a satisfactory resolution.

Teaching, trading, engineering play sessions, gaining access to a group, and consolidating friendships by the exchange of views, plans, memories, and attitudes are some of the uses of talk in the child's social life. There are, no doubt, many others that await our discovery and understanding.

Private talk in a social setting. In the playroom, Judy (31 months) turns to her baby doll while Tom (32 months) plays, a few feet away, with a toy airplane.

Judy

Baby, baby, ba/ . . . What are you gonna do? (*in high-pitched voice*).

Come on . . . Let me tell you something.

Let me tell you something. (*Holds doll and looks at it.*)

I'm going to have some picnic at the table and you'll/ you better be a *good* girl today. (*Looks around at room.*)

Where the table go? ↗ (*Looks at wooden car.*)

Right there, 'kay. (*A question and answer to self, produced in normal voice.*)

Sit right/ . . . (*to doll, putting it on the floor, using higher pitch*).

'Cause I have to take *all* the food and stuff. (*Moves to car and begins to move things off it; resumes normal voice.*)

Don't take Raggedy Ann. Take the trucks off.

And all done (*as she finishes clearing the car*).

(*Mumble.*) Big Teddy bear . . . goes right here. (*Puts the bear on the car.*)

We/ we have to take this Teddy bear.

(*Surveys the car and toys, and after a pause speaks to Tom.*)

Tom, know this/ this / this is a nice/ this is a nice picnic and a nice birthday cake and/ and/ . . . How you feeling, Tom?

7 / Voices

Talk plays a role in the child's acquisition of self and his achievement of social identity. Both these achievements are accomplished with the help of other persons and emerge as the child begins to compare and contrast himself with his familiars and with a widening circle of others. In this chapter I shall explore what the child knows, or comes to learn, of voices; how talk operates to delineate the child's social identity and to classify other persons; and how the child displays and extends his knowledge of social relations and person properties through talk, especially as he tries on the social identities of different persons in pretend play.

To the child, from a very early age, the caregivers' voices seem to be an intrinsic aspect of their presence, although mother's voice does not always sound exactly the same. Sometimes it is soothing and comforting, sometimes exciting, with an element of fun and games, and sometimes it is sharp enough to stop the child short in his tracks, signaling danger or anger. Nonetheless, the voice is hers, and father's voice is his. Although father's is quite different from mother's, it tends to vary just as greatly and to change in similar ways, so that the child learns to predict the weather of his social climate from their voices as well as from their facial expressions. By their third year children reflect not only their own emotional states, but also their sensitivity to the communicative context by such vocal modifications as whispering, whining, speaking very softly, or with distortions in timing or pronunciation. Within the following year they will have a wide repertoire of vocal effects for special purposes and will use these effects in increasingly conventional ways. The child will whisper, for instance, when he is not supposed to be talking, as when he wants to say something to his mother while she is speaking on the telephone or to visitors, or for imparting secrets or other confidential information. The child will use clusters of vocal and verbal modifications in speaking to special types of persons, to babies, for example, as I shall discuss below. Heightened pitch is almost always used in speaking to babies, and many children also raise the pitch of their voices when they speak to their pets or other small animals.[1]

Caregivers may name some of these vocal effects for the children, as Sarah's mother did one morning when Sarah was feeling a bit unpleasant: "I can't understand you when you whine." Judy sometimes lapsed into "fuzzy" and distorted enunciation, and her mother would say: "Why are you talking like that? You sound silly." Children with infant siblings who watch their parents' attention to the new baby with some jealousy have been observed to revert on occasion to babyish pronunciation and talk, hoping, perhaps, to recapture thereby some of the attention that babies obviously elicit. The caregiver may react, saying, "You're talking like Baby Sue. You're not a baby anymore." The child thus becomes familiar with the various uses of vocal modulations and with the signal functions of modifications to mark both the speaker's attitude and the particular communicative situation. At the same time his own voice, with its range of variations, is an intimate part of his very own self. A boy expressed his concern to his partner in the playroom, a concern she apparently shared:

Boy (53 months)	Girl (57 months)
If I grow up my voice will change, and when you grow up your voice will change. (*Slight pause.*) My mom told me. Did your mommy tell you?	
	No. Your mommy's wrong. My voice, I don't want it to change (*sigh*). Oh, well.
Oh, well. We'll stay little, right?	

NAMES AND KINSHIP

In the very complex task of acquiring a social identity, one of the first steps is learning one's name, but even that may not be simple. Children have an "everyday" name that their parents use for general purposes, which may or may not be a diminutive form of their given name, such as Ronnie for Ronald. A young child often has a name for himself that is his own version of his given name, such as Nila for Nigel or Neo for Steven, but this transitional form usually disappears quickly as the child learns the adult pronunciation. He may also have a pet name, used by parents and relatives to indicate affection or playfulness. (An older child who has such a name may insist on discarding it by adolescence, along with other vestiges of childhood.) Parents and other adults often use the child's different names to signal the nature of an upcoming interaction. A child, if addressed as "Miss Muff," "Maggie," "Margaret," or "Margaret Anne Foster," can make a reasonably accurate prediction of the nature of the next message.

The young child must also, of course, learn his surname as part of his identification with his family. Between the ages of two and three, children take part in "name drills" in which they must produce their whole name and the names of mother, father, and perhaps other close relatives. At 25 months, Sarah was confronted with the distinction between role relationship and name. She was already interested in people's names, knew the names of several family friends and her babysitter, and had just learned the name of the observer who was recording Sarah's play with her mother.

Sarah	Mother
(*Turns from observer to mother.*) And your name is Mommy.	
	No, that's not my name. What's my name?↘
Mommy.	
	(*Laughs.*) No, that's my job.
Wh/ What is your name?↘	
	What *is* my name?↘
What's your name?↘	
	I don't know. What's my name?↘
Helen.	
	Yeah.
Daddy call Mommy.	
	No.

At 30 months Jack knew his family name but was still using his own immature version of his first name and found it difficult to name his mother correctly. One of his training sessions, greatly abbreviated in the following excerpt, focused on the names of the whole family.

Jack	Mother
	What's mommy's name? ↘
Henry.	
	Mommy's name? ↗
Yeah.	
	I think that's daddy's name. Daddy's name is Henry.
Yeah.	
	What's mommy's name? ↗
Mommy French.	
	What? ↗ Mommy French? ↗
Yeah.	
	Well, that's pretty close. My name is Alice.
Alice. Alice French.	
	That's right. Jack's name is Jack French.

First, then, the child sorts out the names of the nuclear family. Two-year-old children know the names of their infant siblings, and those who exhibit affectionate behavior toward the infants, also often call them by diminutives when trying to engage the infants in play—Gramie for Graham, or Kay-Kay for Kate.[2] Grandparents are particularly likely to have a label idiosyncratic to the family and the child, such as Pappap for grandfather; uncles and aunts may have pet names as well, Nunkie Ned for Uncle Edward. Judy at 28 months was not clear about the gender component of *uncle* and *aunt* and spoke of her Aunt Leah as Uncle Leah, a mistake her mother immediately corrected. It's a wise child that knows his own kin and, of course, families are quite concerned about the child's identification of persons within the immediate, and often in the extended, family circle. But even when the child is able to name or address his kin appropriately, "Aunt Leah" is at first just a name, as "Grampa" or "Gramps" is just a name, albeit perhaps a very special one. Children only gradually come to understand fully the meaning of kinship terms and how the terms classify persons on the dimensions of sex, generation, consanguinity, and the legal ties of marriage. The terms combine concepts of gender, a dichotomous distinction that is salient to the very young child, and basic relational concepts such as *parent of* and its converse, *child of*.

Age is not a defining characteristic of English kinship terms, but for the child a person's age (relative to himself) is a very salient feature. Although in actual fact aunts and uncles, for example, may be younger than the child, it is very likely that for most young children age enters into their concepts of kin, with aunts and uncles being "old" and grandparents being very old indeed. Relative age among siblings is of major importance, and the child may refer to his older sibling as "big brother" before he can accurately report that he himself is thus necessarily a brother. But many terms in the kinship network involve more distant relational concepts as well as some limited options—an uncle may be either father's or mother's brother—and the terms involve reciprocal relations that do not necessarily involve the child himself in a focal position; for example, the only way a man can be a grandfather is by having a grandchild; or if person A is B's cousin, B is also A's cousin. It is not surprising then, that even nine-year-olds still fail to understand a number of terms in this very complex system of person classification, as Susan Haviland and Eve Clark found in their study of children's comprehension of this network of concepts and terms (experts in linguistic semantics disagree as to the best way of describing the components of meaning that the network comprises).[3]

For the young child, what is at first most important is to acquire those terms that place members of his family in relation to himself; *mommy* and *daddy* are more important than *husband* and *wife*. He must then begin to place himself. His social identity includes not only his name but also his relationships. Even a child of barely three years with a newborn sibling will struggle with this new aspect of identity, announcing, "I sister." Children at this age are quite secure, of course, in the understanding of who is "my mommy" and "my daddy," but even older preschoolers do not fully understand the reciprocal term *son* or *daughter*. It is certainly a relationship they themselves figure in, but perhaps because they do not have anyone in their everyday affairs whom they would call "my son" or "my daughter," the terms remain poorly defined. Although personal experience with relatives may influence the learning of terms at first, it is interesting that later acquisitions are not dependent on the child's actual array of relatives.[4] He comes to understand the concept of *cousin* or *nephew*, for example, whether or not he is one or has one. And he learns that the system of classification works in the same way for anyone, for any family, not just his own. *Mommy* and *daddy*, as might be expected, are the first relational terms that the young child learns to apply correctly to other families. Judy, Tom, Jack, and Anne referred to one another's parents as "your mommy" and "your daddy," although they also used the parent's proper name, for example, Mrs. French, both in addressing and in referring to the friend's mother.

The child's acquisition of kin terms, which occurs over a number of years, is an example of a very common phenomenon in child language and talk. The child uses terms relevant to his own concerns in ways that are often correct and functionally appropriate, but his understanding of those terms may be rather different from an adult's understanding, and the concept that the term (word, phrase) selects may match the adult concept on only one or two of its essential features.

GENDER

A fundamental dimension of the self-concept and of the social identity is that of gender. Long before the child begins to talk, indeed, even from birth, he experiences the multiple ramifications of this distinction, which extend to the ways he is handled, spoken to, and played with, even to the decor of his crib and room. When the child does begin to talk, he is expected to know what he is, and since his caregivers repeatedly tell him, it is not surprising that the two-year-old is generally clear about his appropriate gender label. At about the same time the child learns his own gender, he begins to classify others on this dimension. It is not known precisely what cues the very young child uses to determine the gender of other children—perhaps voice quality, hair length, or clothing, but in many cases two-year-old boys and girls are very similar in these respects. Judy, for example, had shorter hair than Tom, she usually wore pants or overalls, and our observers could not always distinguish their voices without viewing the videotape. We suspect that verbal labeling by adults, which is the most consistent information available to the young child, is the primary cue they use at first. (Various other attributes and indicators of gender then become more differentiated over the next several years.) Those labels come to influence the perception of other gender-related attributes. Preschoolers shown the same infant labeled at one time as a boy and at another time as a girl will maintain that the "boy" is strong, a hearty eater, and active and that the "girl" is delicate, pretty, and fussy.

If there is an infant sibling in the family, a little boy knows if the baby is a boy "like me" or a girl; parents make a point of the fact. Two-year-olds will often volunteer the contrastive information about self and sibling, as did a boy (26 months): "Me boy. Joyce girl. Joyce baby," demonstrating that he could classify the sibling by age/size and gender and could provide the proper name. In their study of young children with younger siblings, Judy Dunn and Carol Kendrick observed that children of this age were also sufficiently confident of their knowledge of the gender of self, sibling, and parents to play with these identifications, as the following excerpt from their records indicates.[5]

Girl (26 months)	*Girl's father*
(Playing with her teddy bear.)	
Teddy's a man.	
	What are you?
You're a boy.	
	Yeah. What are you?
A menace.	
	Yeah, a menace. Apart from that, are you a boy or a girl?
Boy. *(Laughs.)*	
	Are you? What's Trevor? *(referring to the younger male sibling).*
A girl. *(Laughs.)*	
	You're silly.

This child probably did not really need the instruction that was playfully concealed in her father's responses, but the fact that she initiated the topic, as two-year-olds frequently do, suggests that this principle of person categorization was of interest to her. In her initial comment she was, perhaps, extending the principle to determine whether it was applicable to stuffed animals as well. Playful misapplication of gender categorization becomes quite common around the age of three.[6] (Among four- and five-year-olds who are learning the skills of teasing and how delightful the effects can be for the teaser and how distressing for the victim, willful misnaming of gender is a proven technique.) In the following episode Judy's rhythmic, chantlike production and her smile indicated that she was not making a mistake, although Tom was at first surprised at Judy's claim to be a boy. (The length of the pause before a following response is given in seconds in parentheses after the message.)

Judy (31 months)	Tom (33 months)
I'm a / I'm a Indian. I'm a big boy. (1.1)	
	You're a Judy girl. (1.3)
You a big girl? (0.9)	
	No, *you're* a big girl. (0.9)
You a big girl? (0.4)	
	I'm a big *boy*. (1.3)
I'm a big girl. (0.6)	
	I'm a big boy. (0.4)
I'm a big girl.	

This episode illustrates the general tendency, particularly striking in children's talk, for newly acquired skills, concepts, and words to be used as a resource for play.[7] It also exemplifies the use of another dimension of person classification that is interwoven in the child's conceptualization of his own and others' social identities—that of relative age.

AGE, SIZE, AND OTHER DIMENSIONS

People come in different sizes and ages. Chronological age is important to children and their parents, and a self-respecting three-year-old will readily answer even a strange adult's typical question: "And how old are you, little boy?" The pairs of children we observed in the playroom commonly compared ages, exchanging such socially relevant information as the following. A: "I'm four today." B: "I'm already four. Four. That much" (holding up four fingers). But even more important is sorting persons into the relative categories of maturity that the social group recognizes as determining factors in assigning prerogatives and responsibilities, such as baby, child, big boy/girl, teenager, adult/grown-up. Achieving the transition from one of the lesser states to a more advanced and prestigious one is a dynamic aspect of the formation of social identity. Although Judy (29 months) was probably remembering and repeating something her mother had said to her recently, she provided Tom with some important information about herself as they played in her room. Her announcement had nothing to do with the topic of their play.

Judy (29 months)	*Tom (31 months)*
I'm not a baby anymore.	
	You are the baby anymore?
I'm not a baby anymore. No, I'm a big girl.	

This exchange took place just two months before the previously cited playful interchange. A few months later the two children demonstrated that they were aware of the contrast between the categories of child and adult and that they actually had more than one term with which to specify the distinction. The children were in the playroom, and Tom asked Judy where his mother was. Judy reassured him that she was nearby, "finishing her coffee" (which was the explanation the mothers gave the children for their absence from the playroom). Tom, not knowing that the mothers were watching the proceedings from the next room, assumed that his mother was downstairs, where the mothers had coffee when the children were at the co-op playgroup to which they belonged. Tom went on to tell himself that he couldn't go downstairs, and Judy, who was listening, replied.

Tom (33 months)	Judy (32 months)
Can't see her. Ya can't go downstairs, cu / cu / cuz only grown-ups can go downstairs.	
	Hmmm?
Only grown-ups can go downstairs.	
	Only / only grown / only big people can.
Only big people.	
	Yep. Only Mrs. Upton and my mom. (Mrs. Upton is Tom's mother.)
I have Mrs. Upton mom.	

Among the numerous practical considerations that make these stages of maturity salient to the child are the expectations and judgments of others as to what the child can and should do. Caregivers and teachers quite frequently express these judgments, "Big boys don't cry" or "When you grow up, you can have a motor bike." And children are constantly formulating the anticipated joys that a future stage of maturity promises, "When I'm bigger, I can wear high heels, too." Even very young children are aware of some of the practical uses of persons at different stages of maturity. During a play session with her friend Becky, Sarah (26 months) realized that she had a problem and turned from the puzzle they had been constructing to the adult observer, saying, "Tie my shoe." Although Becky was eight months older, Sarah knew, without first making a request of Becky, that the grown-up was the one for this job. C. P. Edwards and Michael Lewis studied the abilities of three- to five-year-olds to place photographs of themselves and of other people into age categories. Children consistently discriminated children from adults and distinguished the transition boundaries at approximately the following ages: between little children and big children, age five; between children and grown-ups, thirteen; between parents and grandparents, forty. When asked to tell whom a child in a story would select to do particular activities, preschoolers chose older friends for teaching, adults for helping, and peers or older children for playing. Boys tended to see children a little older than themselves as suitable playmates, but girls preferred same-age playmates.[8]

Concepts about persons, their relations to oneself and to others are necessarily very complex, involving a variety of integrated dimensions. Many of the dimensions of person categorization are also applicable to other domains of meaning, some primarily to animate entities, such as gender or *mother of*, and some applicable to both animate and inanimate entities, such as *big/little* or *tall/short*. Not only must the child acquire these concepts, but he must learn how his language matches words to them, for the meaning of a word and a concept is not isomorphic. Children gain an adultlike understanding of such common terms as *big girl*, the more difficult person comparisons, such as "I'm bigger than you are," and even more difficult ones, such as "He's younger than I am," but in most cases, this understanding comes a few years after they can confidently express, as Judy did, such an emotionally charged claim as "I'm not a baby anymore. I'm a big girl."

Stan Kuczaj and Amy Lederberg conducted several studies to learn how children between the ages of three and a half and six and a half understand the terms *younger* and *older* as applied to persons. They found that the children varied considerably in their grasp of these terms, but some confusions, as well as some steps in progressing toward understanding, were consistent. In one immature type of response children tended to equate the meanings of *older* with those of *bigger* and *taller*, terms that have more directly perceptible dimensions. But children take different routes to understanding words. Some children interpreted both *older* and *younger* as if they meant *taller*; they may have grasped the idea that the first two terms had something to do with age but did not recognize the nature of their contrast or even that they contrast at all.[9] A child's understanding of these terms, and of many others as well, is influenced by the context in which he hears them. Not all of his caregiver's talk will provide him with unambiguous models, as Martha Robb and Catherine Lord discovered in a study of mothers' uses of the terms *big* and *little* to children younger than 30 months. One mother affectionately told her son that he was "his mother's big little helper."[10]

OTHER VOICES

In the process of sorting out other persons and their properties and learning how persons are similar to one-self in some ways and different in other ways, the child comes to associate certain aspects of voices and ways of talking as particularly appropriate for certain persons and for certain categories of persons. He learns, for example, that if he wishes to engage his younger sister's attention, get her to look at a toy or stop fussing, he will have more success if he raises the pitch of his voice, exaggerates his intonation, and repeats short, simple messages, "Look. Look. Lookie here, Amy. Lookie here. See this? See this?" These are techniques that appear to work quite well with Amy when used by their parents.

Talking to babies in this way does have immediate, sat-isfactory results, but it is also a conventional way of talk-ing to babies, one that adult males and females, whether or not they are parents, invariably adopt with an infant or very young child.[11] Children begin to acquire this speech register, often called "motherese," at about the age of three or four. Children who have watched adults inter-acting with babies (or children whose mothers have en-couraged them to produce this register, as I shall discuss below) probably learn some of its salient features earlier than children who have not had that opportunity. In any case the young child's production of this register is at first somewhat inconsistent and does not include as many typical features of the register as adults' production. Heightened vocal pitch, however, is the first and most consistently used feature, and short utterances with con-siderable repetition and heightened stress are also com-mon. Use of exaggeration in pitch and timing, frequent use of questions, endearments, special baby-talk words and a tendency to use nouns instead of pro-forms are added as the child becomes more fluent in motherese and uses it in a more mature manner.[12] This cluster of features does not occur in the child's speech to peers nor to adults or older children. It is reserved for babies and other entities that the child classifies in the baby category. For many children these include dolls and even stuffed animals if they are functioning for the child as a "baby."[13]

Different types of persons and, more important, the different types of relationships they bear to the child are major determinants of alternative variants in talk, a point previously made in respect to the selection of directive options. The goals of talk are characteristic of the types of persons in particular relationships. The basic dimensions of gender, age or relative maturity, and kinship are associated in a multitude of ways with the interpersonal attitudes and with the characteristic activities persons typically direct toward one another. The vocal and verbal features of talk display and support the essential social knowledge the child is acquiring about himself and others. Babies are relatively helpless and must be nurtured; they are distractible and their attention must be captured and structured; they must be urged to comply; and they need help in understanding. The four-year-old is superior to the baby in all these respects, and his talk to baby affirms that he knows this. In fact, a child's talk may often reflect social knowledge and discriminations of socially relevant attributes of persons and situations that he could not, if asked, "explain" or otherwise articulate. For this reason investigators have looked at children's role play and other pretend activities to learn what they know and think about others and about social situations, knowledge that in their everyday life they may have little or no opportunity to display.

Talking with others' voices.   When children first begin to pretend, at about two years, they start by recreating little bits of their own familiar actions, taking them out of context. A common make-believe gesture is pretending to take a drink from an empty cup or lying down and pretending to go to sleep. But pretending soon involves other persons. The child will pretend to give baby doll a drink or put it to bed or perhaps try out a more complex action, such as putting the doll up to the shoulder and patting it, as if burping it. Mothers of little girls are generally quite supportive of this kind of early "mothering" play. They model the behavior, demonstrating with a doll and adding the characteristic motherese talk, replete with affective expressions of comforting and sympathy, little crooning noises such as "aaaw." Soon little girls are producing a stream of mother patter to their dolls, talk that can be classed as nurturing, controlling or disciplinary, entertaining (singing snatches of nursery songs, for example), and informative or instructive, all produced in the motherese register.[14] Although resembling adult mothers' talk in the ways mentioned above, this talk is the child's imaginative creation, an exploration of mothering. For example, dolls are often disciplined with excessive sternness or anger and are almost always addressed as "Baby," not by name as in real motherese. Although little boys tend not to produce such talk and mothering behavior to dolls, they do understand it and are often interested in what a little girl is doing with her baby doll.

By the age of three, children are able not only to enact the talk of mother, but actually to pretend that they are Mother. They begin to role play, trying on the characteristics of another person and, as an intrinsic part of the other's nature, the voice. The classic formula of person transformation, "I'll be the mother and you be the baby," is the usual prelude to an episode of role play. Interestingly, the voice of Baby is pitched even higher than that of Mother, but Baby usually talks very little. Sometimes Baby can only say "gaa" or "goo-goo." If the Baby is represented as a young child, she often whines and is otherwise very demanding, "I want my teddy bear" or "I want some milk." The pretend Child says "no" quite often in response to a Father's or Mother's directives, expresses displeasure by saying "waah," and indicates petulance by speaking with marked nasalization, lengthening stressed vowels. The pretend Child addresses the Parent as "Mommy" or "Daddy," as appropriate, and is called not "Baby" but usually "Sweetie" or some other endearment. The first pretend roles are those of the nuclear family and are almost always apportioned among playmates along sex-appropriate lines. If no one wants to be Baby, which is common, then a doll can be relegated to the role, and the playmates can be two friendly Mothers who alternately fuss over their (doll) Babies and go about their chores or take their Babies to the park and discuss plans for the day, as did Judy (34 months) and Anne (37 months) during a play session. The two Mothers, when speaking to each other, abandoned their motherly voices.

Even at the ages of three to five, Mother's role in her relationship to Baby or Child is represented more fully both in verbal and in nonverbal behavior than is that of any other member. Father, when he speaks to the Child, uses a gruff voice, deep in tone, and usually louder than either Mother's or the Child's. These qualities not only characterize Father, but are consonant with his role activities: when he is at home rather than "at work," as is usually the case, he must often control and discipline the Child. Role relationships within the family are further indicated by what is said and by the selection of alternative forms of expression. In the role play of three- to five-year-olds, whose capabilities have now expanded to include roles such as Husband and Wife—role relationships they have observed but never occupied in real life—William Corsaro observed a quite consistent differentiation of message types. Family members of superordinate status directed many more imperatives to subordinate members, for example, Mother to Baby, than did Baby to Mother or did members of equal status, such as Husband to Wife. Children requested permission from Parents; Husbands and Wives directed more informative statements to each other than did members in other role relationships.[15]

When children are asked to judge certain words and phrases, they associate them stereotypically with particular adult sex roles, such as "I'll be damned" or "Damn it" with males and "My goodness" or "Oh, dear" with females; these associations are still changing toward the adult patterns of judgment during early adolescence.[16] In pretend play, however, Wives portrayed by four- or five-year-old girls are likely to be excessively polite at a tea party, "Could you just pour me a little bit more?" and they tend to gush a bit over one another's clothes, "Oh, that's *so* pretty." A five-year-old Husband sounded suspiciously condescending when his Wife handed him her earnings: "Why, thank you, honey. You're a *sweet* wife." Perhaps he intended only to be appreciative and fond.

Even more subtle features of the conversational style associated with particular roles and role relationships have been observed in the use of *well* and *uh* as turn holders or markers of a hedged response and of the response variants *yes* versus *yeah* or *yep*. Elaine Andersen asked children between the ages of 45 months and 7 years to provide the voices for puppet characters in three constellations of roles and situations: the family; a doctor, nurse, and patient; and a teacher with two pupils, one a foreign child. In the family situation, Father and Mother speaking to each other or to a Child used *well* to introduce or hold a turn-at-speaking, whereas the Child used the functionally equivalent *uh* to the Parents. Similarly, Mothers and Fathers replied with the more formal *yes* variant, whereas Children used the informal variants in responding to them. Andersen also found that the status relationships of Doctor and Nurse and Patient were consistently marked by a variety of differentially distributed linguistic variants, the Doctor's higher rank being indicated by a deeper voice with deeper and more backed pronunciation of vowels and by less polite directives than the Nurse, whose speech to the Doctor was suitably respectful. The role players even marked the higher status of the Doctor in relation to the Father of a Child Patient by giving the Doctor a deeper vocal pitch and more "dignified" pronunciation.[17]

The question is not how accurate or veridical such role-playing representations really are; as a matter of fact, they are often quite exaggerated and sometimes uneven, and they frequently neglect or distort aspects of the registers used by adults in real life. The role relations of the family and those of sex-role stereotypes are likely to be surprisingly faithful in certain aspects, however. The important point is that such role play displays the children's conception of salient features of person categories and relationships, marking the differences among social types and social interactions. Although there are considerable individual differences in children's participation in social role playing and in their fluency in such activity, children display a remarkable consensus on how any Father or any Mother talks to any Child. It is not specific individuals they represent, but types of persons in types of relationships. The appropriate and differentiating use of voices and styles of talk is as important in the representation of types of social identities in dramatic play as the selection of role-related activities and sequences of events.

FOR MY EARS ONLY

Talking aloud to oneself or to an imaginary interlocutor is frowned upon in adult society, but the child has yet to recognize this constraint. In the first place the young child is not able to "think" silently in words as most adults do, using language to rework a prior conversation, to rehearse, or to try to fix something in memory. In the second place the child, if he is in comfortable and familiar surroundings, has few inhibitions about speaking aloud to express, amuse, or direct himself when the urge arises, whether he is alone or in the company of others. His speech is audible to himself and may be either clear or inaudible (or unintelligible) to others who are present, as it is unconstrained by the transmission requirements of interactive talk. Speech directed to real others, especially when the child desires a response, is as intelligible as the child's ability permits. The variety of vocalizations and talk that emerged from Sarah's room during one nap period (at 28 months) ranged from quiet murmurs to grunts, squeals, and intoned babbles; from humming to snatches of songs and rhymes and counting. It included talk to a doll, a bit of "telephone conversation," descriptions of her own activities, "I'm putting my socks on," and running accounts of her search for and play with toys. The latter varieties were usually fairly intelligible, but they contrasted clearly with her louder and quite carefully articulated announcements to her mother (who was resting in the adjoining room) that she was ready to get up or wanted to go to the bathroom. Most children show a similar range of types of talk for themselves, although they may choose different times or places for such performances. Judy tended not to talk when she was alone in her own room at nap time or bedtime or, if she did, it was too quiet for us to record. Often, however, she would settle down in a corner of the room where her mother was working or in a nearby room and talk, sing, or hum as she played alone with dolls or other toys. Many children tend to specialize in one or another variety of talk for self at different ages.[18] We might expect that the different varieties of such talk serve different functions for the developing child.

When the child is with others, talk may have social consequences, whether or not the child realizes it at the moment of speaking. When two or more children are together in a room, each engaged in his own line of activity, one child's audible comment may be heard and responded to, thus precipitating a talk engagement, or at least a verbal exchange, as was described in Chapter 6 in the discussion of studies by Grace Shugar. Children tend to monitor one another's activities, at least within their peripheral attention. Sometimes the speaker may intend to solicit the other's attention or, at least, he may welcome it. At other times the speaker is indifferent or even resistant to sharing his talk and activity. In one play session Becky was engaged in her own pretend scenario with a doll, speaking alternately to her Baby and to herself—the busy, somewhat preoccupied Mother. Sarah (27 months) was watching, listening, and trying to follow the action. Several times she jumped into a gap in Becky's

talk to ask "What?" ↗ or "What did you say?" ↗ Each
time Becky would reject Sarah's attempts, saying, "I
wasn't talking to you" or "I was talking to my baby, not
you," and then resume her private flow of talk for her
own and Baby's benefit. Children's tendency to talk
aloud about their activities, to describe, plan, and comment on the situation, does, however, make it possible
for other children present to understand what the player
thinks he is doing and to join in if it proves to be interesting.

Children in nursery school may be seated around a
table together, each pursuing a project and a line of talk
related to it, each paying, at least ostensibly, little mind to
any other child's talk. Such apparent cacophony has been
called "collective monologue" and has been considered
an index of childhood egocentrism.[19] Now, however, the
occurrence of such egocentric speech, in which "every-
one talks and no one listens," as Piaget described it, is
thought to be influenced to some degree by the situation.
It occurs more often when more than two or three children are in proximity and are each busy with an independent activity supervised by an adult who is readily
available to discuss it with the child. When two or three
familiar children are alone together, monologues do arise,
but the partner is more likely to share in talk and to be
responsive and attentive to the other, especially when the
speaker's message is audible and intelligible.[20]

There are different kinds of acommunicative speech,
which I define as talk not directed to another actual person. New kinds of acommunicative vocalization and talk
are added in the period from late infancy to early elementary school, and at any age there are considerable individual differences in the amount of such speech. Prior
to the onset of language, most infants babble. Older in-

fants seem to enjoy exploring their newly discovered vocal capabilities and to be learning how they can control the production of sounds. Toward the end of the first year, the child begins to produce more discrete sounds, which resemble syllables and which can be repeated, and vocal contours that resemble some of those of the language he will acquire.[21] He begins a period of producing jargon, elaborate experiments with intonation and nonsense words, and can sometimes be overheard engaging in linguistic practice. William and Theresa Labov discovered their daughter working on a new sound that was not yet a part of her phonological system. She was getting the feel of the *l* sound, producing tokens that were similar to those that only a month later appeared in her speech in the word *apple*.[22] More private practice continues after the child begins to talk, and this extends to grammatical constructions and to the meaning and form of words.

In one of the first studies of this area Ruth Weir found that her two-and-a-half-year-old son Anthony, alone in his room at bedtime, indulged in at least three kinds of private speech.[23] He played with sounds as if he were intrigued by the possibilities of rhyme, alliteration, and onomatopoeia. And he conducted language drills, systematically substituting words, building up and varying linguistic constructions. Ruth Black compared the talk of a child at 26 months and at 28 months in two situations, alone in a crib and in interaction with the mother. She found that the child practiced possessive constructions alone before using them consistently and correctly in the interactive talk situation. An example she provided is similar to Anthony's solitary practice and shows several variations around the possessive construction. (Only part of the example is reproduced here.)[24]

and his eyes
Mammy's eyes
and Mammy's eyes
and precious eyes
and Fred's eyes
and Mommy's eyes
and Nannee's eyes
Mommy's eye and Mommy's (vowel sound)
Tatia's eye and Tatia
Tatia's eye
Tatia's eyes
Tatia's ears
Tatia's lips

Such language practice usually occurs only when the child is alone, but play with nonsense words, rhymes, and real or invented songs occurs in both solitary and social situations. Singing seems to be especially contagious in a social situation; when our two-year-old friends were together, if one began to sing, the other invariably began a song too, but not necessarily the same one. These types of talk can actually be used in social interaction and produced as a collaborative venture.

A third type of acommunicative talk produced by Anthony (and by Sarah, Judy, and Jack) when alone retains a number of features of its source in communicative speech. It makes sense, it exhibits coherence and cohesive ties, and in some cases it takes on the form of dialogue. Children recount to themselves events of the past day, little narratives of what happened or what might have happened. Very often they construct dialogues, with questions and answers, statements and responses. The creator of the dialogue provides the conversational contributions of each person.

Talk to fantasy characters, to dolls, toy animals, and

imaginary (or real, but absent) friends, and narrations to one's self continue through the preschool period and beyond. In these imaginary conversations the speaker roles are usually differentiated considerably. The child splits himself into two or more different characters and gives each speaking role its own voice. The child may take part as himself or function as a narrator/director of the make-believe action and/or adopt one of the pretend roles himself. This kind of talk generally displays normal sentence structure, turn-taking, dialogic exchange patterns, and even terms of direct address for the other roles; and both roles may be produced with considerable expression and dramatic flair. The child is responsible only to himself during such talk, however, and these private dialogues may break off at any point or may rapidly alternate, especially in younger children, with snatches of song, language practice, jargon, mumbles, or uncategorizable noises.

What are the functions of such profligate private talk? The different varieties are likely to have different functions, of course, but as children differ considerably in the amount and types they produce, it is difficult to demonstrate that such talk is essential for development. Some reasonable hypotheses, however, are the following. Language practice, whether of sounds, words, or grammatical constructions, probably gives the child an opportunity to concentrate his attention and efforts on linguistic elements he is just beginning to notice and is ready to acquire. Such opportunity does not occur in the otherwise-motivated and rapidly moving conversational exchanges with other persons. Later, solitary experimentation with linguistic forms and new and interesting meanings may assist the child in becoming more aware of the structures and combinatory potential of his language.

Playful experimentation, unencumbered by interactive demands, may contribute to the growth of metalinguistic awareness, that is, the ability to distance oneself from the immediate use of language and to attend objectively to its form or meaning, isolating and manipulating, for example, some aspect of linguistic structure. Some degree of metalinguistic awareness is required for reading, spelling, writing, and other operations performed on language. Solitary narrations allow the child to remember and, perhaps, to modify experiences, and telling stories to oneself probably summons up for many children the pleasant event of the bedtime story. Making up imaginary dialogues simulates social interaction and provides company when one is alone and, like narration, gives free rein to the creative urge to reproduce, shape, and change reality.

Still another type of acommunicative speech differs in form and probable function from those discussed above. That is the talk a child directs to himself as he is engaged in some motor activity, some task or project. This has been called self-regulatory or self-directive speech.[25] There are two ways that talk may regulate action for the child. The act of speaking itself has rhythmic properties; placement of stress and direction of pitch movement can match or parallel other physical behavior. Counting rhymes or jumprope rhymes are highly institutionalized varieties of talk that accompany and regulate physical behavior for the older child, much as chanting "*da*-da, *da*-da, *da*-da" may accompany the young child's banging of a toy or bouncing up and down. Vocalizing as a motor behavior seems to mesh easily with other kinds of action, and the act of speaking may impel and support motor behavior, quite independent of the meaning of what is said.

Talk can also regulate or shape action through its meaning. As the young child comes to understand the relation between words and their meanings, those meanings can affect behavior. The very young child, in fact, tends to produce action appropriate to a word when that is possible. Marilyn Shatz has shown that on hearing a "do-able" word the two-year-old is likely to act, either not understanding or not attending to the word's linguistic context.[26] This action bias might lead the child to execute a little jump, regardless of whether his mother said to him, "Will you jump for me?" or "The cow jumped over the moon," or whether he heard her say to his father, "If you start now, you'll get a jump on the traffic." With fuller understanding of the linguistic structure and intent of the message, this tendency is soon inhibited.

Before discussing how the meaning of talk comes to direct and regulate behavior, I should note a use of talk that falls between the motoric effects and the meaningful use of talk in regulating action. That use is the marking of boundaries of activity, which is common in both self-directed and other-directed speech. As he begins a new segment of activity, the child will say, "now," and at its end, "there" or "all done," thus verbally punctuating the boundaries of what he sees as a coherent unit, in much the same way that adults, both parents and teachers, organize tasks for children (and sometimes for themselves, as well, saying, "Now then. Let's clean up this mess").

The two-year-old who jumps when he hears his mother utter the word or follows an adult's command of "Put it there," which is very probably accompanied by a pointing or showing gesture, perhaps to a piece and its proper location in a puzzle, is being directed by the speech of others. The meaning of the message influences his action, which follows the message in time. Over the next year the child discovers that by talking he, too, can direct himself to act and then follow those directions. He can direct his own attention by words and can use words to help himself remember or organize what he is doing. Very often this self-regulating speech appears in phrases rather than in complete sentence form; the child may omit subjects and other words that encode information given in the context and in his actions. Three- and four-year-olds are quite versatile: they can describe aloud to themselves what they have just done, can direct themselves in advance of an action, or can provide a running account during the performance of an action or completion of a project. They can suit the words to the actions or suit the actions to the words. The type of activity in which the child is engaged influences the amount of acommunicative speech he produces and its timing in relation to the activity.

Kenneth Rubin and Louisa Dyck listened to the talk of twenty children between three and a half and five years, each of whom was given a number of different toys to play with alone. While a child explored the new objects, he was likely to ask himself questions, such as, "What's this for?" or make comments on the toys during his activity, "Big, big truck." While he was in transition from one activity to another, he tended to give himself directions before undertaking a new project. While actually engaged in building or constructing something, he tended to comment on the materials or on the action itself, "That goes here" or "Don't work right." If dramatic play occurred, the talk appeared less often to serve self-regulatory functions and included more instances of sound effects, expressive utterances, and fantasy statements.[27]

Saying what he is doing as he is doing it even facilitates a child's motor behavior at this period, and the more difficult the task the more helpful it is likely to be. Over the next year, however, this tendency to talk aloud in describing, planning, or executing action, at least during a task assigned by an adult, begins to decline, reappearing at full strength only if the problem or situation is difficult.[28] Under most circumstances the five-year-old relies on verbal and nonverbal thought to plan and organize his activity, to solve problems, or to help himself remember what to do. What others first did for the child, and the child next learned to do for himself, speaking aloud as did others, he has now learned to do for himself with the help of a silent voice.

References
Suggested Reading
Index

References

1 / The Nature of Talk

1. Michael Halliday, *Explorations in the Functions of Language* (London: Edward Arnold, 1973), pp. 9–21.
2. See, for example, Alan Cruttenden, *Language in Infancy and Childhood* (New York: Saint Martin's Press, 1979); and Peter de Villiers and Jill de Villiers, *Early Language* (Cambridge, Mass.: Harvard University Press, 1978). Also recommended is Paul Fletcher and Michael Garman, eds., *Language Acquisition* (New York: Cambridge University Press, 1979).
3. John Austin, *How to Do Things with Words* (New York: Oxford University Press, 1962).
4. John Searle, *Speech Acts* (New York: Cambridge University Press, 1969).
5. H. P. Grice, "Logic and Conversation," in P. Cole and J. L. Morgan, eds., *Syntax and Semantics*, vol. 3, *Speech Acts* (New York: Academic Press, 1975).
6. Harriet Rheingold, "Little Children's Participation in the Work of Adults, a Nascent Prosocial Behavior," *Child Development*, 1982, 53, 114–125.
7. Lois Bloom, Lorraine Rocissano, and Lois Hood, "Adult-Child Discourse: Developmental Interaction between Information Processing and Linguistic Knowledge," *Cognitive Psychology*, 1976, 8, 521–552.
8. Herbert Clark and Susan Haviland, "Comprehension and the Given-New Contract," in Roy Freedle, ed., *Discourse Production and Comprehension* (Norwood, N.J.: Ablex Publishing, 1977), pp. 1–40.
9. David Crystal and Derek Davy, *Investigating English Style* (London: Longman, 1969).
10. Shirley Heath, "What No Bedtime Story Means: Narrative Skills at Home and at School," *Language in Society*, 1982, 11, 49–76.

11. Esther Goody, "Towards a theory of questions," in E. Goody, ed., *Questions and Politeness: Strategies in Social Interaction* (New York: Cambridge University Press, 1978), pp. 17–43.

12. Alicia Lieberman, "Preschoolers' Competence with a Peer: Relations with Attachment and Peer Experience," *Child Development*, 1977, 48, 1277–1287.

13. Edward Mueller, Mark Bleier, Joanne Krakow, Katherine Hagedus, and Paulette Cournoyer, "The Development of Peer Verbal Interaction among Two-Year-Old Boys," *Child Development*, 1977, 48, 284–287.

2 / The Transmission System

1. Erving Goffman, "Replies and Responses," *Language in Society*, 1976, 5, 257–313.

2. Marilyn Merritt, "Repeats and Reformulations in Primary Classrooms as Windows of the Nature of Talk Engagement," *Discourse Processes*, 1982, 5, 127–146.

3. Emanuel Schegloff, "Sequencing in Conversational Openings," *American Anthropologist*, 1968, 70, 1075–1095; and Emanuel Schegloff and Harvey Sacks, "Opening up Closings," *Semiotica*, 1973, 8, 289–327.

4. Emanuel Schegloff, Gail Jefferson, and Harvey Sacks, "The Preference for Self-Correction in the Organization of Repair in Conversation," *Language*, 1977, 53, 361–382.

5. Herbert Clark and Eve Clark, *Psychology and Language: An Introduction to Psycholinguistics* (New York: Harcourt Brace Jovanovich, 1977).

6. Catherine Garvey, "Contingent Queries," in Michael Lewis and Leonard Rosenblum, eds., *Interaction, Conversation, and the Development of Language* (New York: John Wiley & Sons, 1977), pp. 63–94.

7. Tanya Gallagher, "Contingent Query Sequences within Adult-Child Discourse," *Journal of Child Language*, 1981, 8, 51–62.

8. Carole Petersen, Fred Danner, and John Flavell, "Develop-

mental Changes in Children's Responses to Three Indications of Communicative Failure," *Child Development*, 1972, 43, 1463–1481.

9. Harvey Sacks, Emanuel Schegloff, and Gail Jefferson, "A Simplest Systematics for the Organization of Turn Taking in Conversation," *Language*, 1974, 50, 696–735.

10. Stanley Feldstein and Joan Welkowitz, "A Chronography of Conversation: In Defense of an Objective Approach, in Aron Siegman and Stanley Feldstein, eds., *Nonverbal Behavior and Communication* (Hillsdale, N.J.: Lawrence Erlbaum Associates, 1978), pp. 329–378.

11. Candace West and Don Zimmerman, "Women's Place in Everyday Talk: Reflections on Parent-Child Interaction," *Social Problems*, 1977, 24, 521–529.

12. Nancy Ratner and Jerome Bruner, "Games, Social Exchange, and the Acquisition of Language," *Journal of Child Language*, 1978, 5, 391–402.

13. Catherine Garvey, "Some Properties of Social Play," *The Merrill Palmer Quarterly*, 1974, 20, 163–180.

14. Catherine Garvey and Ginger Berninger, "Timing and Turn Taking in Children's Conversations," *Discourse Processes*, 1981, 4, 27–57.

15. Susan Ervin-Tripp, "Children's Verbal Turn Taking," in Elinor Ochs and Bambi Schieffelin, eds., *Developmental Pragmatics* (New York: Academic Press, 1979), pp. 391–414.

3 / Tracking and Guidance

1. Ron Scollon, *Conversations with a One Year Old* (Honolulu: University of Hawaii Press, 1976).

2. Martin Atkinson, "Prerequisites for Reference," in Elinor Ochs and Bambi Schieffelin, eds., *Developmental Pragmatics* (New York: Academic Press, 1979), pp. 229–250.

3. Anat Ninio and Jerome Bruner, "The Achievement and Antecedents of Labelling," *Journal of Child Language*, 1978, 5, 1–15.

4. David Messer, "The Episodic Structure of Maternal

Speech to Young Children," *Journal of Child Language*, 1980, 7, 29–40.

5. Anat Ninio, "Picture-Book Reading in Mother-Infant Dyads Belonging to Two Subgroups in Israel," *Child Development*, 1980, 51, 587–590.

6. Hazel Emslie and Rosemary Stevenson, "Preschool Children's Use of the Articles in Definite and Indefinite Referring Expressions," *Journal of Child Language*, 1980, 8, 313–328.

7. David Warden, "The Influence of Context on Children's Use of Identifying Expressions and References," *British Journal of Psychology*, 1976, 67, 101–112.

8. Elinor Ochs and Bambi Schieffelin, "Topic as a Discourse Notion: A Study of Topic in the Conversations of Children and Adults," in Charles Li, ed., *Subject and Topic* (New York: Academic Press, 1976), pp. 335–384.

9. Peter Lloyd and Michael Beveridge, *Information and Meaning in Child Communication* (London: Academic Press, 1981).

10. Sam Glucksberg, Robert Krauss, and E. Tory Higgins, "The Development of Referential Communication Skills," in Frances Horowitz, ed., *Review of Child Development Research*, vol. 4 (Chicago: University of Chicago Press, 1975), pp. 305–346.

11. Kenneth Kaye, *The Mental and Social Life of Babies: How Parents Create Persons* (Chicago: University of Chicago Press, 1982), quotation, p. 234.

12. Rosalind Charney, "Speech Roles and the Development of Personal Pronouns," *Journal of Child Language*, 1980, 7, 509–528.

13. Christine Tanz, *Studies in the Acquisition of Deictic Terms* (Cambridge: Cambridge University Press, 1980), examples, pp. 67–68.

14. Michael Halliday, "Development of Texture in Child Language," in Terry Meyers, ed., *The Development of Conversation and Discourse* (Edinburgh: Edinburgh University Press, 1979), pp. 72–87; example, p. 81.

15. Thomas Thieman, "Imitation and Recall of Optionally

Deletable Sentences by Young Children," *Journal of Child Language*, 1975, 2, 261–270.

16. The data reported in this study are taken from Joanne Bitetti (now Capatides), "Ellipsis in Children's Discourse: A Descriptive Analysis" (master's thesis, Department of Psychology, The Johns Hopkins University, 1978).

17. Catherine Garvey and Valerie Greaud, "Factors Influencing the Form of Continued Nominal Reference in Children's Talk" (paper presented to the Fifth Annual Boston University Conference on Language Development, October 1980).

18. Barbara Lust and Cynthia Mervis, "Development of Coordination in the Natural Speech of Young Children," *Journal of Child Language*, 1980, 7, 279–304.

19. Ann Eisenberg, "A Semantic, Syntactic and Pragmatic Analysis of the Acquisition of Conjunction," *Papers and Reports on Child Language Development*, August 1980, *19*, 70–78.

20. Ann Eisenberg, "Some Comments on the Acquisition of Linguistic Particles" (unpublished manuscript, University of California, Berkeley).

4 / *The Facilitation System*

1. Roger Brown and Albert Gilman, "The Pronouns of Power and Solidarity," in Thomas Sebeok, ed., *Style in Language* (Cambridge, Mass.: MIT Press, 1960).

2. John Austin, "A Plea for Excuses," in *Philosophical Papers* (Oxford, Oxford University Press, 1961), chap. 8.

3. Charles Ferguson, "Baby Talk in Six Languages," in John Gumperz and Dell Hymes, eds., The Ethnography of Communication," *American Anthropologist*, 1964, *66*, 11:103–114.

4. Erving Goffman, *Relations in Public* (New York: Harper and Row, 1971).

5. Robin Lakoff, "The Logic of Politeness: or, Minding Your P's and Q's," *Papers from the Ninth Regional Meeting of the Chicago Linguistic Society* (1973), pp. 292–305.

6. Jean Berko Gleason and Sandra Weintraub, "The Acquisi-

tion of Routines in Child Language," *Papers and Reports on Child Language Development,* 1975, 10, 89–96.

7. Roger Bakeman and John Brownlee, "Social Rules Governing Object Conflicts in Toddlers and Preschoolers," in Kenneth Rubin and Hildy Ross, eds., *Peer Relations and Social Skills in Childhood* (New York: Springer-Verlag, 1983).

8. Grace Shugar and Barbara Bokus, "Children's Discourse and Children's Activity in the Peer Situation," in Edward Mueller and Catherine Cooper, eds., *Process and Outcome in Peer Relations* (New York: Academic Press, in press).

9. Susan Ervin-Tripp, "Is Sybil There? The Structure of Some American English Directives," *Language in Society,* 1976, 5, 25–66.

10. Claudia Mitchell-Kernan and Keith Kernan, "Pragmatics of Directive Choice among Children," in Susan Ervin-Tripp and Claudia Mitchell-Kernan, eds., *Child Discourse* (New York: Academic Press, 1977), pp. 189–210.

11. William Labov and David Fanshel, *Therapeutic Discourse: Psychotherapy as Conversation* (New York: Academic Press, 1977). See especially chap. 3.

12. Marilyn Shatz, "On the Development of Communicative Understandings: An Early Strategy for Interpreting and Responding to Messages," *Cognitive Psychology,* 1978, 10, 271–301.

13. Kenneth Reeder, "The Emergence of Illocutionary Skills," *Journal of Child Language,* 1980, 7, 13–28.

14. Catherine Garvey, "Requests and Responses in Children's Speech," *Journal of Child Language,* 1975, 2, 41–63.

15. Elizabeth Levin and Kenneth Rubin, "Getting Others to Do What You Want Them to Do: The Development of Children's Requestive Strategies," in Keith Nelson, ed., *Children's Language,* vol. 4 (New York: Gardner Press, in preparation). For a detailed review of work on children's directives, see also Judith Becker, "Children's Strategic Use of Requests to Mark and Manipulate Social Status," in Stan Kuczaj, ed., *Language Development: Language, Thought,*

and Culture (Hillsdale, N.J.: Lawrence Erlbaum, 1982), pp. 1–35.

16. Anthony Wooton, "Two Request Forms of Four Year Olds," Journal of Pragmatics, in press.

5 / On Saying, in Effect, "No"

1. Charles Wenar, "On negativism," Human Development, 1982, 25, 1–23, quotation, p. 5.
2. Rene Spitz, No and Yes: On the Genesis of Human Communication (New York: International Universities Press, 1957), quotation, p. 99.
3. Lois Bloom, Language Development: Form and Function in Emerging Grammars (Cambridge, Mass.: MIT Press, 1970). A more recent discussion is Henning Wode, "Four Early Stages in the Development of L I Negation," Journal of Child Language, 1977, 4, 87–102.
4. Roy Pea, "Logic in Early Child Language," Annals of the New York Academy of Sciences, 1980, 345, 27–43; and Roy Pea, "The Development of Negation in Early Child Language," in David Olson, ed., The Social Foundation of Language and Thought (New York: W. W. Norton, 1980), pp. 156–186.
5. Alison Gopnik, "Words and Plans: Early Language and the Development of Intelligent Action," Journal of Child Language, 1982, 9, 303–318.
6. Pea, Logic in Early Child Language, p. 27.
7. Deborah Keller-Cohen, Karen Chalmer, and Jane Remler, "The Development of Discourse Negation in the Nonnative Child," in Elinor Ochs and Bambi Schieffelin, eds., Developmental Pragmatics (New York: Academic Press, 1979), pp. 305–322.
8. Roger Bakeman and John Brownlee, "Social Rules Governing Object Conflicts in Toddlers and Preschoolers," in Kenneth Rubin and Hildy Ross, eds., Peer Relations and Social Skills in Childhood (New York: Springer-Verlag, in press).
9. Jean Piaget, The Language and Thought of the Child (London: Routledge and Kegan Paul, 1959).

10. Helen Dawe, "An Analysis of 200 Quarrels of Preschool Children," *Child Development*, 1934, 5, 139–157.
11. Svenka Savic and Mirjana Jocic, "Some Features of Dialogue between Twins," *International Journal of Psycholinguistics*, 1975, 4, 33–49; quotation, p. 42.
12. Ann Eisenberg and Catherine Garvey, "Children's Use of Verbal Strategies in Resolving Conflicts," *Discourse Processes*, 1981, 4, 149–170.
13. Laura Lein and Donald Brennais, "Children's Disputes in Three Speech Communities," *Language in Society*, 1978, 7, 299–324.
14. Karen Watson-Gegeo and Stephen Boggs, "From Verbal Play to Talk Story: The Role of Routines in Speech Events among Hawaiian Children," in Susan Ervin-Tripp and Claudia Mitchell-Kernan, eds., *Child Discourse* (New York: Academic Press, 1977), pp. 67–90.
15. Peggy Miller, "Teasing: A Case Study in Language Socialization and Verbal Play," *Quarterly Newsletter of the Laboratory of Comparative Human Cognition*, April 1982, 4, 29–32.

6 / The Social Life

1. Susan Donaldson, "One Kind of Speech Act: How Do We Know When We're Conversing?" *Semiotica*, 1979, 28, 259–299.
2. Grace Shugar, "Early Child Discourse Analyzed in the Dyadic Interaction Unit," *International Journal of Psycholinguistics*, 1981, 8, 55–78.
3. Anca Nemoianu, *The Boat's Gonna Leave: A Study of Children Learning a Second Language from Conversations with Other Children*, vol. 1 in the series *Pragmatics and Beyond* (Amsterdam: John Benjamins B. V., 1980).
4. Elinor Keenan, "Conversational Competence in Children," *Journal of Child Language*, 1974, 1, 163–184.
5. Catherine Garvey, *Play* (Cambridge, Mass.: Harvard University Press, 1977). See chaps. 5 and 6.
6. Susan Iwamura, *The Verbal Games of Pre-School Children* (London: Croom Helm), 1980.
7. William Corsaro, "We're Friends, Right?: Children's Use of

Access Rituals in a Nursery School," *Language in Society*, 1979, *8*, 315–336.

8. Zick Rubin, *Children's Friendships* (Cambridge, Mass.: Harvard University Press, 1980), quotation, p. 102.

9. Catherine Emihovich, "The Intimacy of Address: Friendship Markers in Children's Social Play," *Language in Society*, 1981, *10*, 189–199.

10. Martha Putallaz and John Gottman, "Social Skills and Group Acceptance," in Steven Asher and John Gottman, eds., *The Development of Children's Friendships* (Cambridge: Cambridge University Press, 1981), pp. 116–149.

11. David Forbes, Mary Katz, Barry Paul, and David Lubin, "Children's Plans for Joining Play: An Analysis of Structure and Function," in David Forbes and Mark Greenberg, eds., *Children's Planning Strategies*, in the series, *New Directions for Child Development* (San Francisco: Jossey-Bass, 1982), pp. 61–79.

12. William Corsaro, "Friendship in the Nursery School," in Asher and Gottman, *Development of Children's Friendships*, pp. 207–241; quotation, pp. 221–222.

13. Helena Schwartzmann, *Transformations: The Anthropology of Children's Play* (New York: Plenum Press, 1978). See especially chap. 8.

14. Denis Newman, "Ownership and Permission among Nursery School Children," in Joseph Glick and Alison Clarke-Stewart, eds., *Studies in Social and Cognitive Development* (New York: Gardner Press, 1978), pp. 213–249.

15. Jaipul Roopnarine and Tiffany Field, "Play Interactions with Friends and Acquaintances in Nursery School" (unpublished manuscript, University of Miami, 1981).

16. John Gottman and Jennifer Parkhurst, "Developing May Not Always Be Improving: A Developmental Study of Children's Best Friendships" (paper presented to the Biennial Meeting of the Society for Research in Child Development, New Orleans, March, 1977).

17. Vernon Allen, *Children as Teachers* (New York: Academic Press, 1976).

18. Margaret Martlew, Kevin Connolly, and Christine

McCleod, "Language Use, Role and Context in a Five-Year-Old," *Journal of Child Language*, 1978, 5, 81–99.

19. Courtney Cazden, " 'You All Gonna Hafta Listen': Peer Teaching in a Primary Classroom," in W. A. Collins, ed., *Children's Language and Communication*, Twelfth Annual Minnesota Symposium on Child Psychology (Hillsboro, N.J.: Lawrence Erlbaum, 1979), pp. 183–231.

20. Catherine Cooper, Susan Ayers-Lopez, and Angela Marquis, "Children's Discourse during Peer Learning in Experimental and Naturalistic Situations," *Discourse Processes*, 1982, 5, 177–191.

21. John Gumperz and Eleanor Herasimchuk, "The Conversational Analysis of Social Meaning: A Study of Classroom Interaction," in Roger Shuy, ed., *Sociolinguistics: Current Trends and Prospects*, Twenty-Third Annual Round Table (Washington, D.C.: Georgetown University Press, 1973).

22. Elliot Mishler, " 'Won't You Trade Cookies with the Popcorn?': The Talk of Trades among Six-Year-Olds," in Olga Garnica and Martha King, eds., *Language, Children, and Society: The Effects of Social Factors on Children Learning to Communicate* (Elmsford, N.Y.: Pergamon Press, 1979), pp. 221–236; quotations, pp. 233–236.

7 / Voices

1. Thelma Weeks, "Speech Registers in Young Children," *Child Development*, 1971, 42, 1119–1131.

2. Judy Dunn and Carol Kendrick, "The Speech of Two- and Three-Year-Olds to Infant Siblings: 'Baby Talk' and the Context of Communication," *Journal of Child Language*, 1982, 9, 579–595.

3. Susan Haviland and Eve Clark, " 'This Man's Father is My Father's Son': A Study of the Acquisition of English Kin Terms," *Journal of Child Language*, 1974, 1, 23–48.

4. James Chambers and Nicholas Tavuchis, "Kids and Kin: Children's Understanding of American Kin Terms," *Journal of Child Language*, 1976, 3, 63–80.

5. Judy Dunn and Carol Kendrick, *Siblings: Love, Envy and Understanding* (Cambridge, Mass.: Harvard University Press, 1982).

6. Martha Wolfenstein, *Children's Humor* (Glencoe, Ill.: Free Press, 1954).

7. Catherine Garvey, "Play with Language," in Barbara Tizard and David Harvey, eds., *Biology of Play*, Clinics in Developmental Medicine no. 62 (London: William Heinemann, 1977), pp. 74–99.

8. Michael Lewis and Jeanne Brooks-Gunn, "Toward a Theory of Social Cognition: The Development of Self, in Ina Uzgiris, ed., *New Directions in Child Development: Social Interaction and Communication during Infancy* (San Francisco: Jossey-Bass, 1979), pp. 1–20.

9. Stan Kuczaj and Amy Lederberg, "Height, Age, and Function: Differing Influences on Children's Comprehension of 'Younger' and 'Older,'" *Journal of Child Language*, 1977, 4, 395–416.

10. Martha Robb and Catherine Lord, "Early Uses of *Big* and *Little* by Mothers and Children," *Papers and Reports on Child Language Development*, 1981, 20, 108–115.

11. Joseph Jacobson, David Boersma, Robert Fields, and Karen Olson, "Paralinguistic Features of Adult Speech to Infants and Small Children," *Child Development*, 1983, 54, 436–442.

12. Judith Josephson and Johanna DeStefano, "An Analysis of Productive Control over an Educational Register in School Age Children's Language," *International Journal of Psycholinguistics*, 1979, 6, 41–55.

13. Jacqueline Sachs and Judith Devin, "Young Children's Use of Age-Appropriate Speech Styles in Social Interaction and Role-Playing," *Journal of Child Language*, 1976, 3, 81–98.

14. Peggy Miller and Catherine Garvey, "Mother-Baby Role Play: Its Origins in Social Support," in Inge Bretherton, ed., *Symbolic Play: The Representation of Social Understanding* (New York: Academic Press, in press).

15. William Corsaro, "Young Children's Conception of Status and Role," *Sociology of Education*, 1979, 52, 15–79.

16. Carole Edelsky, "Acquisition of an Aspect of Communicative Competence: Learning What It Means to Talk Like a Lady, in Susan Ervin-Tripp and Claudia Mitchell-Kernan, eds., *Child Discourse* (New York: Academic Press, 1977), pp. 225–243.

17. Elaine Andersen, "Learning to Speak with Style: A Study of the Sociolinguistic Skills of Young Children" (Ph.D. dissertation, Stanford University, 1977).

18. Stan Kuczaj, Brooke Harbaugh, Alice Bean, and Rick Boston, "The Developmental Relations of Young Children's Pre-Sleep Monologues and Social Speech" (paper presented to the Biennial Meeting of the Society for Research in Child Development, Boston, April 1981).

19. Jean Piaget, *The Language and Thought of the Child* (London: Routledge and Kegan Paul, 1959).

20. Edward Mueller, "The Maintenance of Verbal Exchanges between Young Children," *Child Development*, 1972, 43, 930–938.

21. Charles Ferguson and Marlys Macken, "Phonological Development in Children: Play and Cognition," *Papers and Reports on Child Language Development*, May 1980, 18, 138–177.

22. William Labov and Theresa Labov, "The Phonetics of *Cat* and *Mama*," *Language*, 1978, 54, 816–852.

23. Ruth Weir, *Language in the Crib* (The Hague: Mouton, 1962).

24. Ruth Black, "Crib Talk and Mother-Child Interaction: A Comparison of Form and Function," *Papers and Reports on Child Language Development*, August 1979, 17, 90–97; quotation, p. 93.

25. Karen Fuson, "The Development of Self-Regulating Aspects of Speech: A Review," in Gail Zivin, ed., *The Development of Self-Regulation through Private Speech* (New York: John Wiley and Sons, 1979), pp. 135–217.

26. Marilyn Shatz, "Children's Comprehension of Their Mothers' Question-Directives," *Journal of Child Language*, 1978, 5, 39–46.

27. Kenneth Rubin and Louisa Dyck, "Preschoolers' Private Speech in a Play Setting," *Merrill-Palmer Quarterly*, 1980, 26, 219–229.

28. Virginia Tinsley and Harriet Waters, "The Development of Verbal Control Over Motor Behavior. A Replication and Extension of Luria's Findings," *Child Development*, 1982, 53, 746–753.

Suggested Reading

Susan Ervin-Tripp and Claudia Mitchell-Kernan, eds., *Child Discourse* (New York: Academic Press, 1977). One of the first collections of papers on children's spontaneous talk.

Olga Garnica and Martha King, eds., *Language, Children, and Society* (New York: Pergamon Press, 1979). Papers on the influence of social structure and context on talk.

Michael Halliday, *Learning How to Mean: Explorations in the Development of Language* (London: Edward Arnold Press, 1975). Essays dealing primarily with functions of language in the very young child.

Eleanor Ochs and Bambi Schieffelin, eds., *Developmental Pragmatics* (New York: Academic Press, 1979). A collection of papers on the topic of language use.

Iona Opie and Peter Opie, *The Lore and Language of School Children* (Oxford: Clarendon Press, 1960). A compilation, with very insightful discussions, of the rhymes, riddles, chants, charms, and jokes that children have created and perpetuated over generations.

John Sinclair and R. M. Coulthard, *Towards an Analysis of Discourse: The English Used by Teachers and Pupils* (London: Oxford University Press, 1975). A description of classroom talk.

Gordon Wells, ed., *Learning through Interaction: The Study of Language Development* (New York: Cambridge University Press, 1981). Papers detailing the relations of language structure to language use. See especially the chapter by Gordon Wells entitled, "Becoming a communicator."

Index

a/the, 66

Acommunicative speech, 53, 209–215; in infants, 209–210; as language practice, 210–211, 212; self-regulatory, 213, 215. *See also* Private speech

Action, 214; requests for, 109, 113–124; conversation and, 156–157

Action bias, 118, 214

Action lines, 157, 158

Activity space, 107

Addressee: attitude toward, 4; attention and availability of, 32–35, 62, 65; rank of, and RA form, 121–122

Adults, *see* Caregivers

Adult talk: function of, 3; repairs in, 37, 38; turn-taking in, 48; request for action in, 114

Age, 197–200; and kinship terms, 192–193

Anaphoric proword, 64

Anaphoric reference, 60, 80, 86, 87

and, 88

Andersen, Elaine, 205–206

Appreciation of persons, 101, 105

Argumentation, rational, 140–141

Arguments, 141; exchange type, 142. *See also* Quarrels

Article, definite/indefinite, 66

Attention: of addressee, 32–35, 62, 65; of children, getting, 33–34; of teacher, 34–35

Austin, John, 5, 6

Babies, speaking to, 102, 188, 201–202

Back-channel feedback, 36–37

Bargaining, 182. *See also* Trading

because, 135, 136

Black, Ruth, 210

Boggs, Stephan, 150

Bokus, Barbara, 106

Boundaries: marking, 35–36, 214; in turn-taking, 49, 50

bring/take, 72, 76

Bruner, Jerome, 63

but, 90–91

Caregivers: cooperation with, 10–11; turn-taking and, 50–52; temporal patterning and, 53; child–caregiver games, 50, 63; and ritual conventions, 105–106, 108; use of RA options, 117–118; as teachers, 173–175; voice of, 187–188. *See also* Fathers; Mothers

Causal relations, 89, 90

Charney, Rosalind, 74–75